Strength to Care

Reflections for Parents of Children with Complex Medical and Special Needs

Kevin M. Troupe

Printed in the United States of America
ISBN-13: 978-1514354261
ISBN-10: 1514354268

Dedication

This book is dedicated to my wife, Theresa, who has always been my number one fan and supporter. You have cheered me on in victories, held my chin up in failures and believe in me before I believe in myself. There is no way I could explain on paper the ways you hold our unique family together. You are a wife, a mother, a nurse, a pharmacist, an advocate, a teacher, a baker (not a cook), a scheduler, and above all, a person who seeks the heart of Jesus. I am humbled to be given such a person to share this walk with.

Acknowledgements

My Family—Hannah, Megan, Matthew, Sarah Anne and Isaac. I thank God that he thought so highly of me to bless me with and trust me to be your earthly father. I am humbled each day as you strive to be the person that God has designed you to be and as you chase the dreams he has placed in each of your hearts. I also thank you for allowing me to share our ups and downs with other people who are hurting.

My Church Family—Thank you for modeling what the hands and feet of Jesus looks like here in this world. You have been constant in loving us, praying for us and providing for us during this journey we are on. I never cease to be amazed at how God can place a need on your heart even before the need is spoken. You have sat with us in waiting rooms, your prayers have carried us through tough times, meals have nourished us when we were weak and in each step we have taken we know we have never walked alone.

Lessons from Matthew & Isaac Followers—Thanks for being a part of our family and supporting us along the way. Thanks for being gracious as I have been vulnerable and have shared our joys and sorrows with you. I am always encouraged in each step knowing that you are there and are praying for us.

Supporters of this book project—Special thanks to Judi Warner and Pastor Steve Gibson who read and shared their comments on early drafts. Thanks to Lynda Freeman who helped me with content editing even while you are busy with your own projects and family. Thanks to Alyssa Helm who dissected my words and challenged me to dig deeper in areas that were weak. Your polishing made my thoughts and stories look better and have more meaning in word form.

Introduction

THERESA AND I were married on a beautiful fall day in October of 1991. We selected a Bible verse for the front on our invitation that we both believed in.

A cord of three strands is not quickly broken.
Ecclesiastes 4:12

What we didn't know as we said our vows is how those strands would be stretched and tested during the journey we were about to begin.

God has blessed us with five beautiful children. Hannah will be 21 in the fall, Megan turned 19 in the spring, Matthew just turned 14, Sarah Anne will be six this summer and Isaac turned three as summer began. If you are doing the math in your head you may recognize the gaps. We certainly have—and there are explanations that go with them. The explanations center around a random mutation of gene CHD7, located on the long arm of chromosome #8, more commonly referred to as CHARGE Syndrome. It is rare, it is not gender specific and the odds of having two in one family are even rarer.

Matthew and Isaac have both been diagnosed with CHARGE Syndrome. There are many medical and behavior anomalies associated with a CHARGE Syndrome diagnosis, but even with a diagnosis, the label does not define them. The gaps widened between our kids as we came to terms and embraced the challenge of raising one, now two children with special needs.

This book is not about CHARGE Syndrome or about any other diagnosis or label. It is a look into our lives of living with two boys who happen to have some special needs. There are many books, journals, papers and studies *about* what our boys *have*. This book is more about what we can learn *from* who our boys *are*.

I started sharing stories of our journey over five years ago in a blog title *Lessons from Matthew*. At first I thought sharing our story was a creative expression and a way to help others. What I have found it that it helps me just as much. It helps Theresa and the rest of our family reach out and see people, hurting people more clearly and it helps to put our own struggles into perspective. In return, we are strengthened. We have become a voice of hope and encouragement as we talk and interact with doctors, nurses, caregivers and to the groups we have been asked to speak and share our story with. We have spent countless hours in surgery waiting rooms, much more time, measured in days and months in hospital rooms and immeasurably more hours with caregivers and nurses in our home over the past 14 years sharing our faith in words, but even more importantly in our actions and in serving through a listening ear and through loving people right where they are at. As it often turns out, we have been blessed just as much as Matthew and Isaac have touched many lives and have been embraced by thousands as they have laughed with us, cried with us and prayed us through each step of their lives.

The "lessons" you are about to read are in no particular order of time or in theme. They are just in the order as God put them on my heart to share. They all have the common theme of a hospital stay, surgery, complication or just plain old life is really hard right now. It is our prayer that our journey encourages you and gives you strength to care more deeply and with more understanding as you take care of the ones who have been placed in your care.

Contents

Willing or Unwilling?

I THINK I am safe to assume most of us would not rank a visit to the dentist as one of our favorite things to do. The annual or semi-annual ritual of having your teeth cleaned can put even the hardiest person on edge. After all, the visit really is a report card on the progress of our daily regime of brushing, flossing and avoiding the sweets…or lack thereof. Personally, I have experienced the good and the bad of a visit to the dentist. The bad included the final demise of a tooth which had a root canal many years ago, cracking in half years later and finally progressing to the point where it had to be pulled. Many of you may be squirming in your chair at this point. I have to admit; it makes me uncomfortable even thinking about it.

Why would I talk about such an uncomfortable subject? Well, it reminded me of a visit to the University of Michigan Dental Clinic to get Matthew's teeth cleaned. There was no way to prep Matthew for this visit. He simply did not understand it was for his own good…yeah, we have all heard that before. "It is for your own good." Or "This will hurt me more than it will hurt you." A trip to the dentist for Matthew either includes sedation, which is not always a good thing for him, or the dreaded Papoose Board, a device which straps his body to a board so his arms and legs cannot hurt the person, or people, working on him. Matthew hates this Papoose thing, though he does recover quickly. As soon as the Velcro is undone, he is back to the normal Matthew.

After this visit, I pondered the whole dentist experience and how very different it was for Matthew another time when we made an emergency visit to our local dentist. Matthew was constantly pulling at a tooth that was being pushed out by his adult teeth coming in. It was being pushed out at a grotesque angle and appeared to be incredibly painful. After many attempts to take care of it on our own, we finally scheduled an office visit. It took only a few minutes, with no sedation, numbing or Papoose board, to pull the tooth out. Matthew was quite eager to allow the dentist to remove the tooth, even guiding the dentist's hands to his mouth. As soon as the tooth was gone, Matthew was giddy and happy as he carried and played with his little tooth box for the rest of the night.

These stories are a strange contrast of visits to the dentist, one a willing visit; the other not so willing.

This is similar to various situations when God is at work in our lives. Sometimes, when we are hurting or have an intense focus on a situation or event in our lives, we willingly go to our Father and ask for His help and beg for Him to do something to make the pain go away. Yet other times, we sit back wonder why God allows bad things to happen and run their course. In those times, it seems as if God cannot hear you, or is just not listening. Those times are our unwilling visits, when the Father is at work, shaping and forming us. The tough times are for our own good, helping make us better, stronger people.

> *Consider is pure joy, my brothers and sisters, whenever you face trials of many kinds, because you know that the testing of your faith produces perseverance. Let perseverance finish its work so that you may be mature and complete, not lacking anything.* ***James 1:2–4***

I have to admit, the words "pure joy" aren't the first to come to my lips when I am facing a trial. With experience, though, comes wisdom, and as I get older I would like to think I am becoming more mature. The following quote is a great companion to the words from James:

3

"Character cannot be developed in ease and quiet. Only through experiences of trial and suffering can the soul be strengthened, vision cleared, ambition inspired and success achieved." **Helen Keller**

I read an analogy a few months ago about how when we intervene with nature, even when we think we are doing something good, it can have devastating results. The illustration focused on how the butterfly breaks open the cocoon and enters the world. If you watch a butterfly do this, you might want to help, as it can take hours for the process to happen. You might just want to peel back the cocoon and release the butterfly, but doing so would not only be tragic, it would be fatal for the butterfly. You see, it is through the struggle of breaking apart the cocoon that the wings are strengthened and the butterfly is able to fly.

So, when you face your next trial, what will it be? Willing or unwilling? Most of the time, it is just a matter of attitude.

Prayer: *Lord, please help me to face challenges willingly, using the situation to teach me and shape who I am. Help me to understand that the easy way* *out of a situation is not always the best for me. Much like the butterfly gains its strength from the struggle to be free from the cocoon, strengthen me as I go through a trial knowing I will be able to spread my wings in the end with confidence and endurance for the next trial. Amen.*

Preparing the Way For Extraordinary Destiny

"Hardships often prepare ordinary people for an extraordinary destiny." **C.S. Lewis**

LAST YEAR, WE were able to move to a new home that Theresa says gives her a feeling of peace. The safety and function factors we added to an already great layout were: biometric fingerprint scanners on all exterior doors, key code locks on many interior doors, double-hung windows which all open at the top, a new "sanity wall," as we call it, which separates the main floor in two halves; this slows down Matthew's access to the kitchen, dining room, Isaac's room and the laundry room. We also added French doors to keep Matthew from accessing the foyer which has stairways to the upper and the lower levels.

The whole process of looking for a new home, securing it and the actual move was somewhat of a dream come true. For several years, as Matthew grew older, wiser and more talented at locks, gates and other means of keeping him safe, it was apparent we needed to make some significant changes...either to the existing house or to start looking at other options as far as our home was concerned. Then, along came Isaac! Another "hardship," although an adorable, sweet one, launched us into another realm of needed changes!

Here is where the rubber meets the road (Caution: vulnerability here exposing weakness; not for the faint of heart). We were in no financial position to consider a move. We were three years into our Dave Ramsey plan of becoming debt free, just being able to keep our heads above water and not living paycheck to paycheck. I did carpentry work on the side, at least up until Isaac was born. All of this money went to pay down debt and get us closer to being able to make a move in the direction of a new home. As we were approaching the light at the end of the tunnel, along came Isaac. With the combined needs of Matthew and Isaac, we faced the reality of needing to make significant upgrades and repairs to the current house, which would have been nearly impossible to do with Isaac in the house, due to his trachea tube (air quality, dust, etc.). Moving out and then making the repairs would have been cost prohibitive, not to mention we needed a bigger house than the one we had with a workable floor plan...one which allowed for safety and function.

This is where my prayer life was centered, when it was not focused on surgeries, healing, milestones and just plain life in general. Another vulnerability alert here, my prayer was usually filled with doubt. I felt like we were being blessed beyond measure just to sustain us, keep us strong and healthy and able to face each new challenge. People responded to needs we never expressed...something only God could arrange. How could I possibly ask for more? In my own reasoning, I thought I would leave the miracles of healing and a little help here and there with the bills to God, but I was convinced the debt thing and the housing thing were my own problems and that I needed to work for them. After all...my mess, my problem. I didn't feel worthy of an extraordinary destiny.

"The greatest tragedy of life is not unanswered prayer, by unoffered prayer." **F.B. Meyer**

Thankfully, I have people who are always praying on behalf of my family and a wife who was praying for a solution, with much more expectancy and frequency than I was. With the assistance of two different non-profits, we were able to make a move quicker than we ever dreamed possible. And it was easier than having to make needed repairs on our old house. We were also able to make the modifications we needed to bring our new home into a safe and functional state. I am at a loss for words to describe how in awe of God I am, for how He prompts people, and how they not only listen, but respond in ways I could never imagine. What would God have done if I had the faith to actually ask? It is a good thing I am at a loss for words, because the two non-profits who assisted us have asked to remain anonymous. A selfless act of love prompted by God alone, because I was too weak and filled with doubt to ask.

A Prayer for the Ephesians:
For this reason I kneel before the Father, from whom every family in heaven and on earth derives its name. I pray that out of his glorious riches he may strengthen you with power through his Spirit in your inner being, so that Christ may dwell in your hearts through faith. And I pray that you, being rooted and established in love, may have power, together with all the Lord's holy people, to grasp how wide and long and high and deep is the love of Christ, and to know this love that surpasses knowledge—that you may be filled to the measure of all the fullness of God. Now to him who is able to do immeasurably more

than all we ask or imagine, according to his power that is at work within us, to him be glory in the church and in Christ Jesus throughout all generations, for ever and ever! Amen.
Ephesians 3: 14–21

There is so much to grasp in this prayer, this letter from Paul to the Ephesians. We have personally experienced and are still grasping "how wide and long and high and deep is the love of Christ." We have also been witness to what "immeasurably more than we can ask or imagine" looks like in real life!

What hardship can you prayerfully hand over? What is your extraordinary destiny? I am learning that my destiny is not in the hard work I do or my lame attempts to earn God's favor. My destiny has everything to do with grasping how wide and long and high and deep His love is for me.

Prayer: *God, help me to understand and grasp how wide and long and high and deep your love is for me. Make the inadequacies I feel be overcome by your love for me so I can confidently ask and know you will respond. God, I allow you to dwell in my heart to face hardships, knowing that each one prepares me for an extraordinary destiny. Amen.*

Strength to Care/Troupe

Do We Know His Voice?

IT NEVER GETS easy. Isaac was scheduled for a third cleft repair surgery; the one that would focus on his lip and nose, with a slight touch-up on his palate. It was not easy to plant the last kiss and give the last squeeze of the hand as the anesthesiologist team wheeled him down the hall.

As we prepared for another surgery, you might think that with our nearly 40, yes 40, combined surgeries and procedures between Matthew and Isaac, we would be on cruise control...but, they never get easier. In fact, they get harder. Harder because as the boys get older, they also get wiser and it hurts more. Hurts them more and hurts us more as we sign the next consent form.

Although we enter these new experiences with a healthy respect and are aware of the risks, we also go with a firm belief that everything is in God's hands. You see, we are in tune with a certain voice. A voice which leads us through tough valleys AND beside restful waters.

It is not easy to be tuned in to this voice. There are much louder, much fancier and even sometimes seemingly more logical voices to listen to. We are surrounded by voices which pull us in many directions; unfortunately in the direction of feeling stressed, being anxious, fearful and not at peace.

*My sheep hear my voice; I know them,
and they follow Me.* **John 10:27**

I am sure it was no coincidence I was reading a book that prepared me for this next step of faith. The book is *The Lord Is My Shepherd: Resting in the Peace and Power of Psalm 23* by pastor and author Robert J. Morgan, who is no stranger to caring for sheep. He walked me on a journey through this most famous and most quoted Psalm. As we approached this "valley" and as I kept reading, I was reminded of this thought:

> *"That's the thing about valleys. They have shadows and sorrows, but they are 'through' passages. Psalm 23:4 does not speak of a cave or a dead-end trail. It's a valley, which means it had an opening on both ends...David didn't even use the phrase 'though I walk in the valley'. The emphasis is on through, which indicates a*

temporary state, a transition, a brighter path ahead, a hopeful future."

I think we would all prefer the place of quiet waters and the lush green pastures where we can lay in the sun and have the serene picture of peace. However, we cannot fully experience one without the other. God leads us through both, which means He doesn't prevent us from entering the shadowy valleys, but He does promise to lead us through them, with a little comfort along the way.

Interestingly, the same wooden staff talked about in Psalm 23:4, that gives correction by guiding our paths is the one that reaches out, gently on our backs as an extension of the shepherd to show affection and assurance.

How do we find that voice, that peace? How do we get back on the path? Rob shared this story of a sheep in his flock which was blind due to age:

"Lucy became so old and feeble that she was virtually blind. She often ran into the gate or fence because she couldn't see anything...for all practical purposes, she was blind. Yet there was nothing wrong with her hearing...she wouldn't

move until she heard my voice. But, when I called her, she would always take a tentative step in my direction. I'd have to keep talking to her, because otherwise she'd get off track. She'd go on a wayward course…It's in reading, memorizing, pondering, and searching God's Word that we most clearly hear His voice and gear our minds to His whispers in our ears, telling us when to turn to the left and to the right."

Are you anything like Lucy? Do you get off track? Take time to listen to His voice. Pray for the ability to hear the peace and assurance which only comes from our Shepherd's voice.

Prayer: *Jesus, when I am on a wayward course, help me to slow down enough to hear your calming voice. Guide me through the valleys of my life. Thank you for your gentle voice which leads me out of the valleys into the green pastures and beside restful waters. You are my shepherd. Amen.*

Does God Give Us More Than We Can Handle?

ONE OF THE most used phrases spoken to people who are in the middle of a crisis, struggle or burden is, "God will never give you more than you can handle." Usually this is followed by, "You must be really strong." Those of us who are in the special needs community this is often shared "You must be really special if God has given you such a special one to care for."

These comments are well intended and we do take them as a compliment even though sometimes they can be irritating. I guess it is better than being told, "You had it coming" or "You deserved it." Actually, in not so many words from some well-meaning people, we have been questioned about why we had more kids after Matthew was born. But we were no more likely than any other father and mother to have two CHARGE Syndrome children.

Is it really more than we can handle? Yes, if we choose to handle it on our own. The reference to God not giving us more than we can handle comes from 1 Corinthians 10:13. It says:

No temptation has over taken you except what is common to mankind. And God is faithful; he will not let you be tempted beyond what you can bear. But when you are tempted, he will also provide a way out so that you can endure it.

The first part is often quoted, but not the second. Those who are not familiar with the text, or the fundamental reason for God's gift of His Son, could be left hanging with the question of why God would "give" us a crisis. God doesn't "give" us bad things in our lives. But, when things do go bad, we were designed not to go at it alone. We were meant to have someone walk beside us and give us the encouragement and strength we need to get to the other side of peril. The second part of the text promises God will provide a way out so we can endure it.

It really is more than we can handle—the struggle, the illness, the suffering, the job loss, the bullying or (insert your burden)—if we choose to suck it up and handle it on our own. However, when we embrace the burden and begin to accept help from above and abroad, we develop endurance and later, freedom.

"You must really be special parents if God gave you such special children." Our medically, emotionally, physically and mentally challenged boys did not come with an instruction manual and we certainly do not given super powers to "be strong." We firmly believe each one of our children was gifted to us for specific reasons, certainly not because of our qualifications. It was because of the competency and potential God saw in us. If you need any further evidence, just look at the twelve men who were closest to Jesus. If credentials and a résumé were the only criteria used for their future calling, they wouldn't have even been invited to a first interview. I read a commentary this past week by television personality Mike Rowe, where he mentioned this concept while referring to the process of being hired for his first television gig:

Here's what I didn't understand 25 years ago. QVC had a serious recruiting problem. Qualified candidates were applying in droves, but failing miserably on the air. Polished salespeople with proven track records were awkward on TV. Professional actors with extensive credits couldn't be themselves on camera. And seasoned hosts who understood live television had no experience hawking products. So eventually,

19

QVC hit the reset button. They stopped looking for "qualified" people, and started looking for anyone who could talk about a pencil for eight minutes.

QVC had confused qualifications with competency.

Perhaps America has done something similar?

Look at how we hire help – it's not so different from how we elect leaders. We search for work ethic on résumés. We look for intelligence in test scores. We search for character in references. And of course, we look at a four-year diploma as though it might actually tell us something about common-sense and leadership.

God does not look at what we have done, He doesn't peer at the wall and look for the credentials, and He won't even take time to poll your friends on how nice of a person you are. What He will do is look at your heart. He will look at the gifts and talents you have been given and examine what you have done with those, and your potential to make the best of them. He is also there, right beside you when you face something you think you cannot handle.

As for the critics who have questioned our sanity to have more children, this is between God and us. Yes, it has been and continues to be hard to raise them, keep them safe and keep them healthy. We sacrifice family vacations. We don't get enough sleep. Relationships are fractured. Our germ phobia is misunderstood. The list, which goes on and on, could fill a complete blog post. But we would not change a thing.

We would not change a thing because of the impact suffering and hardships have had on our lives. They have made us better people, better in ways which could never be explained on a résumé.

Prayer: Lord, thank you for the children I have been blessed with to care for. Thank you for the reminders of who is really in control and who gives me the strength and the wisdom to care for these unique gifts from you. Help me to see your unique fingerprints as you walk beside me in this journey. Even though I may not feel qualified at times to embrace these gifts, I know that you have made me competent. Help me to trust in the decisions I make and to continue confidently. In the days when things seem too tough to handle, give me a gentle reminder that I am not in this alone. Amen.

Be Blessed. Be Grateful.
Give Thanks.

EVEN BEFORE ISAAC joined our family, God had already taken us on a path of complete reliance and surrender when we were blessed with Matthew. As we look back at the year before Matthew was born, it is clear God had a plan in mind when we experienced some financial difficulties and I took a "responsible" job, stepping aside from self-employment for what we thought would be a brief time. This was 14 years ago. What began as a job, God used to move us from an already strong faith into a transformation of being broken and rebuilt. It is clear to us now how He was preparing us for a special journey of faith; a journey which would include our church family and beyond.

Some of you reading this have been a part of our journey of being broken and rebuilt. Whether through prayer, helping with caregiving, financial help, providing transportation (literally, in giving us a car), helping with yard work, house work or just sitting with us as we waited out a surgery or hospital stay, you have been there. I wish I could say we have been diligent in thanking each of you personally. We are learning it is a progression of being blessed, feeling grateful and then giving thanks. As we have gone from one crisis to another, we have been woefully short on the "giving thanks" aspect. I know ultimately we give thanks to God, and we do, but it does not excuse us from thanking those He works through. These gestures of selflessness extend way beyond our own family and serve as a continued witness of how God's people care for each other. THANK YOU.

Our recent holiday months were not without trials. Isaac spent a week in the hospital after experiencing some respiratory distress. We discovered he had slight pneumonia, which he was able to fight through and recover from quickly. As we adjusted to "hospital crisis mode," I sat in a dark hospital room listening to the ventilator as it helped Isaac breathe just a few days before Christmas. I could not help myself...I started asking the familiar question of "Why?" Why are we going through this again? I had recently picked up several books. The one I grabbed on my way to the hospital was *The Red Sea Rules: The Same God Who Led You in Will Lead You Out*, another great book by Robert J. Morgan. Rule number two helped me put my whining aside:

Be Blessed. Be Grateful. Give Thanks

Be more concerned for God's glory than for your relief. **Robert J. Morgan**

As I read through the chapter there were stories about facing the storms, how the same God who led you in will continue to lead, how His grace is sufficient; all things which sound oh so familiar in our journey. Once again, I found myself being blessed, feeling grateful and then giving thanks.

It can be hard to explain to people how we can remain so positive when they read about our story and what we have faced, and will continue to face, in raising two boys with a rare genetic disorder. How do we face each day, each setback or illness? Paul explains how I feel much better than my words can:

> *I was given a thorn in my flesh, a messenger of Satan, to torment me. Three times I pleaded with the Lord to take it away from me. But he said to me, "My grace is sufficient for you, for my power is made perfect in weakness." Therefore I will boast all the more gladly about my weakness, so that Christ's power may rest on me. That is why, for Christ's sake, I delight in weaknesses, in insults, in hardships, in persecutions, in difficulties. For when I am weak, then I am strong.* **2 Corinthians 12:7b–10**

We are strong and His power is made perfect primarily because we embrace the fact we are weak. We do not have all the answers, and we do not try to manipulate the outcomes. We accept that our journey has been, and will continue to be, a difficult one. I am not sure I would say we "delight" in weakness and in difficulties, but I will say we accept them and know His grace is sufficient for allowing us to be blessed by weakness and difficulties, be grateful for them and then give thanks.

Prayer: *As Paul mentions, help me to see the "thorn in my side" as an honor to have and to be considered worthy to possess. Help me to know and embrace that my weakness is made strong through your grace. Help me to not only to accept the blessings you provide through help from others but also to be grateful and give thanks. When I feel embarrassed to ask for help, remind me that I am denying the opportunity for others to use the gifts and resources you have blessed them with. Amen.*

Do You Have A Praying Mattress?

I JUST LOVE the innocence of life through the eyes of a four-year-old. One summer a praying mantis took a liking to our front porch. Many times while entering and leaving our front door it was relaxing on a brick-capped wall next to the door. The first time our daughter Sarah Anne encountered this new friend was on the sidewalk along our garage. She came in the house loudly exclaiming, "There is a praying mattress on our sidewalk!"

We have certainly had our moments of needing prayer as Isaac and Matthew grow. Theresa and I have had many long, sleepless nights of prayer on our own king-sized Sleep Number "praying mattress" as we pray those boys and our girls through life. When we see a break between the medical crises in our lives, we have been busy praying other families in our CHARGE syndrome family through their crises. Theresa and I have been both touched and burdened with crying and praying for losses, surgeries, procedures and therapies for our other CHARGE and special needs friends. The "praying mattress" gets a lot of use. We know very well the fragility of life.

Is prayer your steering wheel or your spare tire?
Corrie ten Boom

We have learned over time not to pray for God to fix everything or take away all of our struggles. We have learned that prayer is not the final resort; what we do after all else fails. Rather, prayer should be our steering wheel, guiding our thoughts and our direction. Prayer has a way of helping us refocus and hit the issues in our lives head-on.

> *Peace. It does not mean to be in a place where there is no noise, trouble or hard work. It means to be in the midst of those things and still be calm in your heart.* **Unknown**

On one recent sleepless night for Matthew, I was keeping a listening ear on him as he was awake in his bedroom next to ours. As I lay there, I recalled the end of summer, the transition into autumn and the milestones we have passed with seemingly little fanfare. I rejoiced in the non-events. No hospital stays for Isaac and no major illnesses under our roof. Yes, we have had cares with Theresa's mom and the ever-present vehicle issues, but even those make us feel a little more like a "normal" family. Another huge leap was the fact that Theresa has been able to join a Bible study group on Tuesday mornings, with the help of our church family and much coordination of the Special Needs Ministry. She is able, at least for a few hours each week, to take a much-needed respite from the demands of being a caregiver and a mom.

We are grateful we have had some time to just say thanks for a smooth patch of road. Yes, the Troupe family lives on the edge most of the time. We live lives full of noise (literally!), trouble and hard work. But our focus is to keep prayer as the steering wheel and not the spare tire in the trunk. The next hill is always on the horizon.

Just about the time I was wrapping up my thoughts on this chapter, the Troupe "normal" showed up yet again. On an outing to celebrate Hannah's birthday, Matthew broke the tranquil, meditating stillness of a koi pond at a local mall by pushing Sarah Anne in while she fed the fish. Ah, the memories we create…good times.

Prayer: *God, as I spend time with you in prayer may I focus more on thanking you for being near than on my list of needs. Even in the midst of the next trial, may my eyes be on the lessons learned and the people I come in contact with. Help me to be aware of the example I set and the tone of how I react to what is going on in my life. May my prayer time be more of a steering wheel as I navigate life, rather than using it as a spare tire...only when I am in need. Amen.*

Can Brokenness Be A Gift?

A WEEK CAN see such change. For example, one week we were preparing and packing for our trip to Mott's Children's Hospital for Isaac's stomach surgery. The following week we were all back home and very grateful for how things turned out. Very nice, simple bookends, wouldn't you say? The rest of the story is how God works in and through us while we go through the dark moments of doubt, worry, anxiety, lack of sleep, driving back-and-forth across the state to tend to family, work needs and setbacks—just when you think things are progressing. There is great heartache in watching your precious little one go through pain and wanting to take it away, even for just a few hours.

During that dark week, I could not get out of my head what I wrote in my journal exactly a year ago, as we were fumbling through the first few weeks of Isaac's life. I wrote about a few quotes in a book by Sheila Walsh called *God Loves Broken People.* Here is an excerpt from my journal along with the quotes. I felt it was worth repeating:

"I told her that I still take medication, and every morning I take that little pill with a prayer of thanksgiving that God made a way for those of us who suffer like this on such a broken planet. And, I told her that in the darkest moment of my life, I discovered that God lives very close to the floor, very near to those who are broken." **Sheila Walsh**

While hanging in the abyss of time in a hospital NICU watching Isaac heal, I had the time to finish a few books I hadn't yet finished. The quote above is from God Loves Broken People: And Those Who Pretend They're Not *by Sheila Walsh. This book is a great read and has been perfect for the life we have right now—broken and hurting, but trusting and having hope for an abundant life to come for Isaac. There are many, including us, who are living close to the floor in prayer, right where God meets us.*

We sit with him, and touch him when we can. We beg God to fix him, make him whole, healthy and strong enough to come home. We already love him more than any words can speak. I have to pry Theresa away from that isolette—his little cocoon which has been the only thing he has ever seen in his short life—each night to get the needed rest she needs. After all, she has had major surgery too.

I am being broken in ways too. It has nothing to do with healing, pumps, hoses, ventilators or with this hospital at all. I am struggling with surrendering and allowing people to serve us. Guys just don't handle this well. I am the one who serves people, and our family is the one that hangs around long after an event and picks up the pieces, resets the platform when everyone else has gone home. We are the ones who serve, fix things; we talk to other parents who are struggling with the news of a not-so-perfect child. We are the ones creating the "manual" on how to effectively clean poo from a ceiling fan. We (mainly "I") have a hard time being served...okay, I said it. "My name is Kevin and I have a hard time being served."

While we are tending to Isaac, there is a host of people arranging care for Sarah Anne and Matthew; helping with fundraising to help send Hannah to Mozambique, Africa, and Megan to Marvell, Arkansas, on mission trips this summer; planning and plotting to enter our home and finish my painting project and tackle the huge mommy-is-nesting list I still had six weeks to complete, until last Sunday changed our lives and "our" plan. My family is in shock (I think I even heard a gasp) that I am going to allow someone else to paint in our living room.

Another quote from Sheila's book...more words I needed to hear today:

"What if the brokenness we ask God to fix is in fact a gift? What if the wounds we beg God to heal, the burdens we plead with Him to remove, are the very things that make us fit for His service? Can our brokenness be a blessing?"

I, for one, and the rest of the Troupe clan can answer this question. We are living proof and will testify about how brokenness can be a blessing. I am learning—actually, just starting to learn—how to let go and allow people to serve. I was told a few times this week that if I do not allow people to serve us, I am denying them their blessing of using their gifts, talents and wealth. I would be a stumbling block and deny our church family the opportunity to be a family since families are supposed to care for one another and meet each other's needs.

A repeat of the emotions from a year ago. God still meets us very close to the floor as we beg for Him to take this current pain away. But the floor gives us a perfect point to push off of and get back up. We have found strength in being on the floor, strength to offer other people hope and encouragement to not stay there. Yes, our brokenness, our burdens, our hurt make us fit for His service.

Just a few "coincidences" this past week. I use this word in quotes with a little sarcasm…we know they were not just coincidences. A family we met when Matthew had open heart surgery just "happened" to be there for a third and final surgery for their little girl, which provided a moment for us to lean on each other. On one trip home from the University of Michigan Hospital on the other side of the state, a fellow church member approached me and said, "This has never happened to me before, but I felt like God told me to give this to you." He handed me a $100 bill. He didn't know I needed to fill up the ITV (Isaac Transport Vehicle) the next day to return to the hospital. The exact amount to fill up the tank—yes, $100.

At one point during the week, I stepped out of Isaac's room to stretch my legs. When I returned, Isaac's nurse had been replaced and Theresa was in a very deep discussion with the new nurse. Theresa was sharing her experience of peace when she felt God was telling her this child, this baby in her womb was a perfect fit for our family. This was the morning before we heard the news of how Isaac was not going to be "perfect" according to this world. Theresa filled me in later on how the nurse was pregnant with twins and one had been determined to have a genetic disorder which was "not compatible with life." Doctors told her that the baby would die in the womb or shortly after birth. They talked a lot about grief and pain and all I could think was, "These are the very things that make us fit for His service."

Our family does experience a lot of pain and suffering as we deal with each new challenge, but we also have very strong arms as we have lifted ourselves up off the floor each day. Those strong arms have put us in a very unique position to be able to lift others up as God puts them in our lives. He is glorified in all circumstances…sometimes in the fall, sometimes in getting up and many times as we assist others who need lifting.

Prayer: *Father, I find myself many times on the floor. Thank you for meeting me there when I need you the most. Help me each time to be lifted up, knowing that each time I get up my arms become stronger and I am made even more fit for your service. I pray for opportunities to be able to share my "close to the floor" moments with those who are put in my path who need to know the floor is exactly where you will meet them. Help me to see that the brokenness I face can actually be a blessing...for me and for others. Amen.*

Are You Making Yourself Grumpy?

AS WE WERE all hanging out at home one day, we heard a familiar sound coming from Matthew. Having a child who is non-verbal can be challenging, but we have learned to identify his sounds almost as if they were an assigned ringtone or notification tone on our phone. He was annoyed, which in most cases means Sarah Anne has done something, taken something or is just generally in his peripheral space. Theresa called out the accompanying phrase, "What's wrong with Matt?" Usually this phrase is followed by a confession or an observation by Sarah Anne. This time the response made all of us laugh. She responded with: "I didn't do anything...Matthew is making himself grumpy." We laughed at yet another Sarah Anne original phrase and went on with our day. It wasn't until later that the innocence of this phrase hit me hard.

> *"The pupil dilates in darkness and in the end finds light, just as the soul dilates in misfortune and in the end finds God."* **Victor Hugo – Les Miserables**

Later in the day as I was driving, I began to recall moments God plants in and around the trials we were going through. It's funny how we tend to focus all of our energy on the trials and miss the small rays of sunshine—God's reminders He is silently there, silently giving us everything we need. One such reminder was during an emergency trip across the state to replace a leaking feeding button for Isaac. We were lamenting about our broken central air conditioner back home and the reality we would not be able to afford going to the bi-annual CHARGE Syndrome Conference that year (a much-anticipated, encouraging, recharging event). These things and many more were heavy on our hearts as we entered the hospital, but then God gave us a little oasis in the form of a chance encounter. Theresa accidentally pressed a button for the wrong floor in the elevator, and as the doors opened, there stood another CHARGE Syndrome family we had not spent time with in four years. After our appointments, we had lunch and shared part of the afternoon together. We shared experiences and laughed as we caught up with what had been going on over the past several years. It was a much-needed boost. We felt as if we had a mini conference in just one afternoon.

Life is but a Weaving (the Tapestry Poem)

"My life is but a weaving
Between my God and me.
I cannot choose the colors
He weaveth steadily.
Oft' times He weaveth sorrow;
And I in foolish pride
Forget He sees the upper
And I the underside.
Not 'til the loom is silent
And the shuttles cease to fly
Will God unroll the canvas
And reveal the reason why.
The dark threads are as needful
In the weaver's skillful hand
As the threads of gold and silver
In the pattern He has planned
He knows, He loves, He cares;
Nothing this truth can dim.
He gives the very best to those
Who leave the choice to Him."

Corrie ten Boom

Oh, the times I can relate to this line:
"Oft' times He weaveth sorrow;
And I in foolish pride
Forget He sees the upper
And I the underside."

41

The words, "And I in foolish pride" stick out to me every time I read this poem. I think this is because it cuts right to a central problem I deal with—pride. I don't like to admit that I can't do this on my own, that my family cannot do this on our own. I too often forget that there is an upper side which I may only get to see glimpses of in this life. I have to fight not to fix my gaze on the confusing underside. Each broken vehicle, each leaking pipe, each surgery, each ER visit is just another shuttle making its way through the weaving loom. My foolish pride blurs my vision of how this tapestry is transforming my life and the lives around us. A large part of this tapestry is the people we come in contact with as we ride the shuttle through the loom—the caregivers, nurses, doctors and fellow travelers, along with our family, extended family and our church family. Whether we are being used to lift up and encourage other families or are the receivers of someone's talent, gift or financial help, all of it is part of the tapestry of which we only get to see glimpses. Oh, what a beautiful garment it will be when it is revealed to us in Heaven!

My prayer is that God would help me to fix my gaze on the glimpses of the upper side of the tapestry even though my vantage point is mainly the underside. Oh, and also to not "make myself grumpy" in the process.

Prayer: Lord, help me enjoy the small glimpses of the beautiful garment that is being created in the loom. The bottom view of my life's tapestry can be so confusing and frustrating at times as I struggle to understand the shuttles path. Help me to accept that you have a perfect plan even though it will involve pain and at times not make sense. Lord, I thank you for the "chance" encounters you place in my life to add encouragement exactly when I need it. Amen.

His Name Is Faithful and True

For just as we share abundantly in the sufferings of Christ, so also our comfort abounds through Christ.
2 Corinthians 1:5

PLANNING, SCHEDULING CAREGIVERS, paying bills, packing, more packing and—somewhere between all of this—some nervous anticipation and worry. No, it's not a vacation…

We left in the wee hours of a Monday morning to arrive for Isaac's scheduled surgery at 7:30 a.m. Ugh, that meant a 3:00 a.m. wake up time for travel and pre-op! We asked our prayer team partners to once again storm the gates of Heaven with their prayers for this delicate surgery. Matthew had this same surgery at just a few months old—a Nissen Fundoplication, a procedure on the stomach which eliminated the ability to burp, throw up and reflux. With Isaac, we had to wait until his esophagus was completely healed from a previous surgery and did not need constant dilating (stretching) to stay open. His small stomach was also something which played into the decision to delay this complicated procedure.

The Sunday before we left for the surgery was an emotional and joy-filled day. We spent time with the elders of our church as they anointed and prayed with Isaac before we left for his surgery. They prayed not only for Isaac but for us as a family. It happened to be Mother's Day; Theresa was overcome with emotion as she held Isaac tight, recalling how just the year before she was not even able to hold him on this same day. Another memory came flooding back as we sang "Ten Thousand Reasons (Bless the Lord)" by Matt Redman. We stood arm in arm the year before in church and cried our eyes out as we left our vigil with Isaac, who was just a few days old, to worship and thank God for the journey we were about to begin.

Often we are called upon and moved to pray for other families who are on a similar journey as ours. One morning as I was praying for one of these families I came across these few paragraphs from John Eldredge's book *Beautiful Outlaw: Experiencing the Playful, Disruptive, Extravagant Personality of Jesus*. I shared it with our friends as they sat through a long, third major heart surgery for Paislyn, a.k.a. Little Miss Miracle. After typing it out and sending it along to them, I let it soak in and found it was just as relevant to us.

Your suffering is neither pointless nor isolated. Somehow, Jesus' sufferings overflow into our lives; somehow ours are linked to his. This is a great honor. It grants our sorrows an incredible dignity; it invites us to know an intimacy and connection with Jesus in them, because of them. The sufferings of Jesus are the noblest part of His life story; the cross, the crown of thorns. What an unspeakable honor He would share even this with us. This fellowship is a treasure we have not tapped into, but one we will need.

When His suffering overflows into our lives, God's promise is His comfort will overflow to us as well. We can cry out for the comfort of God. Whatever your circumstances may be, He will heal your wounded heart; He will comfort. Cling to him.

My soul clings to you; your right hand upholds me. (Ps. 63:8).

He is with you now. For His name is Faithful and True.

His name is Faithful and True…oh, how we have found this to be true over the years! Hours upon hours suffering through surgery waiting rooms, bedside in a hospital room and even watching a chest rise and fall as our children peacefully sleep. For some of our children, breathing was natural and easy. We never gave it a second thought. But when Matthew and Isaac were born, each breath, each heartbeat had to be monitored and recorded.

"Faith like Job's cannot be shaken because it is the result of having been shaken." **Rabbi Abraham Heshchel**

We entered the new surgery as we had the dozens past, with faith, knowing God is Faithful and True.

Prayer: *Jesus, help me to see that my suffering is a great honor and is not pointless or isolated. You made the greatest sacrifice and suffered a painful death for me. Help me to see that my suffering is done alongside you. You are with me always. You are faithful and true. Amen.*

What Dog Are You Feeding?

A CONSTANT QUESTION we are asked is, "How are you guys doing?" I know the question is almost always referring to either Isaac and/or Matthew. There are varying degrees in which we answer the question. Isaac's medical needs and Matthew's "creativeness" would bog anyone down if we went in to all the details. Most of the time we keep it to the short version of "good" or "we need prayer." There a few people who are in our tighter circle of friends where the question is more directed to the rest of us…and uncomfortably, toward Theresa and me. I say uncomfortable because we are not always doing fine. It is a hard thing to admit we don't always have it all together.

For those who directly care for a special needs child, a sibling or perhaps an ailing family member or parent, there is a common term called caregiver fatigue. Yep, we have it…a lot. Caregiver fatigue may consist of several things and can be quite varied in intensity. The best way to describe it is the feeling of being trapped. Theresa describes it as feeling like everything ultimately defaults to her; medications, appointments, therapies, consultations, nursing schedules, etc., no matter how much the rest of our family helps with these things, she feels and absorbs the brunt of what doesn't get done. I have the same feelings about being the primary provider for our family. Neither one is more important (or easier) than the other. This is where the trouble can begin.

I am going to be vulnerable here. One struggle within me is the feeling of being "entitled" to take a break when I have just finished a long day at work. I am the provider, but being so doesn't mean my obligation ends when I leave work. I have those kinds of days where I am physically and emotionally exhausted, where I have calculated and conserved just enough energy to make it to the recliner and am ready for my relaxation and break. When I get home, there are times I am faced with the same look from Theresa, the same kind of look in her eyes and an unspoken scream of, "I'm tagging out, and it's your turn." This is the point where I am left—we are left—with the decision of doing the right thing and deciding who is going to be "tagging in." We are both tempted to begin sharing our responsibility lists of the day and compare who has done more or who gets a break first. The competition of who is more deserving of wearing the crown of service. Yes, it is a battle of the flesh.

So I say, let the Holy Spirit guide your lives. Then you won't be doing what your sinful nature craves. The sinful nature wants to do evil, which is just the opposite of what the Spirit wants. And the Spirit gives us desires that are the opposite of what the sinful nature desires. These two forces are constantly fighting each other, so you are not free to carry out your good intentions. But when you are directed by the Spirit, you are not under obligation to the law of Moses. **Galatians 5:16–18 NLT**

Preach it, Paul; I know exactly how this feels. I just finished a book by author and speaker Ken Mansfield titled *Stumbling on Open Ground: Love, God, Cancer, and Rock 'n' Roll*. The book is about Ken's two bouts with cancer and the honest and open discussions he had with his God as he battled through the journey of treatment. He said this about the struggle of doing the right thing:

I am like Paul in that I try to do what is right. I want to be obedient and pure, and yet I have these thoughts; I behave in ways that are outside God's purpose, outside his ways, outside his pleasure. I want to be pleasing to him. I want to be good and godly, but then, like a fool I do the

51

very things that he and I both do not want me to do. I go bonkers with my stupidity and he keeps loving me. What is wrong with this picture? Maybe I should ask myself, what is right with this picture?

"I go bonkers with my own stupidity." Now there is a phrase I can relate to! I get this feeling as soon as I start the caregiver competition of who deserves a break more. And still, "He keeps loving me." I love the story Ken went on to share, a story he heard as he grew up near a Native American Reservation. The story is about faith vs. fear; these two are always at odds, just like doing the right thing vs. doing the wrong thing:

One of the elders from the nearby Nez Perce reservation used to tell the story about an old member of the tribe who had become a Christian. His name was So-bo-ta, and a few months after his conversion he asked the pastor who had brought him to the Lord if he could meet with him. He told the pastor that he was having a hard time dealing with a personal struggle in his Christian walk and that he felt like there were two dogs fighting inside of him. He said one dog's name was Faith and the other dog's name was Fear. He said these two dogs were constantly battling inside him, and it was driving him crazy. The pastor looked at him intently, thought for a minute, and asked, 'Well, So-bo-ta, which dog is winning?' The old Indian squinted his eyes, stared off into space as if watching a movie, and then answered in words so soft that they were almost inaudible: "I guess the one that I feed the most."

Which dog am I feeding the most, the dog of self-centeredness or the dog of selfless service? Do I get it right all the time? Absolutely not.

Theresa and I shared a rare moment this past week. It was a moment when Theresa stepped away from her world of schedules and lists and made a spur of the moment decision. I was working a food event at church for 400 women who were attending a weekend retreat. Megan was asked to dance a ballet number during the evening worship time. Theresa made the decision to load up the three little ones at home (our oldest was away at a 4-H event), along with the needed equipment for Isaac, complete with a nurse, and make it in time to see, video and take photos of Megan. She did it all with about five minutes to spare. Matthew was content, Sarah Anne fell asleep and Isaac had a nurse with him as they waited it out in the car.

There we stood, arm in arm, nearing the end of Megan dancing before the Lord. My face had a smile from ear to ear and Theresa had tears running down hers. In this brief moment in our crazy lives, we rested in our Father's arms.

Not all days are like the struggle I described above; it all depends on which dog we are feeding at the time. Do you have the same struggle of which dog to feed? My prayer is for God to give me the strength and desire feed the right dog.

Prayer: *God, please help me in the times I feel everything defaults to me. Help me when I feel the effects of caregiver fatigue. Give me strength to feed the right dog...the dog of selfless service instead of giving all the attention to selfishness. Even though they may be brief at times, I thank you for the times when I am able to feel the weight of caregiving lifted. Amen.*

"There's A Hole In His Lip?"

WE HAD A very tender moment which reminded us that everything we experience and our subsequent response is entirely influenced by our perspective. What we see with our eyes is not always how we interpret what is before us. Very early on as we embraced the fact Isaac was likely going to be as challenging, if not more than Matthew, we tried to prepare Sarah Anne for the birth of Isaac and how he may look a little different from her little baby dolls. We explained what a cleft was, showed her pictures and shared how Isaac may have to spend some time in the hospital after he was born. None of this really mattered when Isaac joined us. To her he was, "Isaac, my baby brother." Her most used comment: "He's soooo cuuuute!"

We waited and prepared for when Isaac's complex little body, with his many issues, would be healthy enough to begin the process of repairing his cleft lip and palate. The first surgery was for a "nose job" to repair his flat nose and to re-align some of his facial muscles. This was to be the first of three, or maybe four, as they moved from the nose to the palate and then to the lip.

We shared this news with Sarah Anne and excitedly talked about how Isaac was going to have the hole in his lip repaired. Sarah Anne's puzzled response was, "Isaac has a hole in his lip?" Then came the tears as we explained that fixing his lip (and palate) would help him eat and breathe better. Then she started to sob. "But, he's so cute the way he is, I don't want you to fix him!"

> *If you think of this world as a place intended simply for our happiness, you find it quite intolerable: think of it as a place for correction and it's not so bad. Imagine a set of people all living in the same building. Half of them think it is a hotel, the other half think it is a prison. Those who think it a hotel might regard it as quite intolerable, and those who thought it was a prison might decide that it was really surprisingly comfortable.*
> **C.S. Lewis, God in the Dock**

Do you see a setback, a disability, a disfigurement, etc. as a hotel or a prison? I think we are comfortable in saying our family has the perspective, according to the C.S. Lewis quote above, of coming from the "prison" side. We do not think this place is intended for our happiness. If we did, we would be pretty disappointed, as if expecting a glorious hotel. No, we accept this current state as a prison and find many opportunities and moments when it can be surprisingly more comfortable than expected. It is not always easy to see at first, but God's fingerprints are all over the events in our lives, and even though it may seem as if we are in a "prison," His light permeates those walls if we make those walls transparent.

> *There are only three types of people; those who have found God and serve him; those who have not found God and seek him, and those who live not seeking, or finding him. The first are rational and happy; the second unhappy and rational, and the third foolish and unhappy.* **Blaise Pascal**

My prayer is that I will see through different eyes beyond blemishes and see the beauty God has created. I pray that I see beyond the sins of others and love as I am commanded. I pray that my will is conformed to God's will, not the other way around. May my prayer be like Blaise Pascal's:

> *I ask you neither for health nor for sickness, for life nor for death; but that you may dispose of my*

health and my sickness, my life and my death, for your glory...You alone know what is expedient for me; you are the sovereign master, do with me according to your will. Give to me, or take away from me, only conform my will to yours. I know but one thing, Lord, that it is good to follow you, and bad to offend you. Apart from that, I know not what is good or bad in anything. I know not which is most profitable to me, health or sickness, wealth or poverty, nor anything else in the world. That discernment is beyond the power of men or angels, and is hidden among the secrets of your providence, which I adore, but do not seek to fathom. **Blaise Pascal**

Prayer: *God, help me to understand and to embrace the life you have chosen for me. Help me to see this life as a prison and believe that your life and light shines through the walls so I can see that things are surprisingly comfortable instead of quite intolerable. Help me to have eyes like Sarah Anne has...able to see the beauty in things instead of what may be considered unsightly or intolerable in this world. Amen.*

Feeling the Heat, But Not Giving In to the Burn

I WILL NEVER forget a time when I was in the back of an ambulance on the way to the hospital with Isaac. I rhythmically squeezed an AMBU bag, which continued to provide oxygen to Isaac's lungs while the EMT with us in the back called in Isaac's weak vitals and continued prepping him for our arrival at the hospital. Theresa was left behind; a wreck after providing the first 20 minutes of CPR.

Isaac had a good night and was doing fine as I was being briefed by the night nurse and I was about to take over care for him. In a matter of minutes it had all changed and Isaac was turning a shade of blue in color and his right leg began to twitch. I yelled for Theresa and she immediately started CPR as I called for help and the nurse assisted with getting vitals. Our minds raced as we cared for our boy. I will also never forget the glassy-eyed look he had until we made it to the hospital and they took over care.

*In addition to all this, take up the shield of faith, with which you can extinguish all the flaming arrows of the evil one. **Ephesians 6:16***

Our family and our praying family were a witness to the miracle of Isaac surviving a series of seizures brought on by an unexplained loss of sodium in his blood; a loss and level so low we were told by doctor after doctor his level was "too low to sustain life." We experienced many "flaming arrows" around this event in the form of a broken windshield (our Toyota), a dead battery (our Explorer), a broken alternator (on the miracle Suburban donated by a few close friends in response to being prompted in prayer), along with fevers and vomiting on the home front.

After a week in the hospital, we were truly able to see the incredible triumphs and the "flaming arrows" we experienced, an expected result when God has been or is working in a powerful way. Spiritual warfare is a real thing and cannot be dismissed. We have learned, and continue to learn, that we may feel the heat from the flaming arrows, but we do not have to take the bait and experience the burn. Even though it can be hard in the moment, we need to recognize what the real reason may be for the "bad" things that happen.

We had a tough week for sure. I stayed at the hospital at night with Isaac to stay clear of the colds and fevers which were running rampant at home with Theresa and the rest of the family. I woke up every morning from my transformer chair/bed in Isaac's room in the Peds ICU on the eighth floor with a great view of the rising sun. I cannot dismiss the fact that the exact spot the sun rose was directly above the church where we worship, where I work and where our family is blanketed by prayer and blessed with help for our ever-expanding needs. I was overcome one morning with the weight of what had transpired over the previous several days. I reflected while sitting next to Isaac's hospital bed on something Theresa had taped to what we call "the inspiration wall" (a cabinet door in our kitchen). It is a quote which reads:

> *I have learned that in every circumstance that comes my way, I can choose to respond in one of two ways: I can whine or I can worship! And, I can't worship without giving thanks. It just isn't possible. When we choose the pathway of worship and giving thanks, especially in the midst of difficult circumstances, there is a fragrance, a radiance that issues forth out of our lives to bless the Lord and others."* **Nancy Leigh**

DeMoss, Choosing Gratitude: Your Journey to Joy

As I finished my moment of gratitude and praise that morning, and after wiping the tears from my eyes, I set to work on phone calls to the garage and the auto glass company, handled a few things at work and checked in with Theresa who was caring for all the sick ones at home while being sick herself. Isaac's nurse overheard my phone calls while she was sitting in our room doing her charting and asked the question, "How on earth do you deal with all the drama in your life?" I told her all of these little "annoyances" pale in comparison to having to do CPR on your own child and how we are privileged to witness miracle after miracle. A few flaming arrows from the enemy seem like pesky flies. But a good attitude is a moment of fragrance, a radiance issued forth from our lives, from Isaac, to bless the Lord and others. Our next few days with this nurse and others were filled with talking about faith, struggles, healing and how good God is.

God is good, all the time…all the time, God is good.

It doesn't end there…it's never a perfect ending. After just one night home again as a family and looking forward to a long couple of days to catch up on some sleep and healing for the rest of the family, our night nurse called in sick an hour before her shift. Plan B was initiated and once again we were left with the choices of whine or worship. It's never easy, but we will take the miracles over sleep anytime.

Prayer: Lord, help me to understand what it truly means for you to be in control of everything. Also, when you are working in mighty ways, help me to recognize that the fiery darts that come my way are just mere annoyances and can easily be fended off with your shield. Let me experience the heat but not to give into the burn. I can whine or I can worship...lead me into worship. Amen.

Our Two Special Needs Kids Have Wrecked Our Lives

DID THE CHAPTER title grab your attention? Good, because it was meant to, but not in the way you may be thinking. Sure, I could go down the path of, "why me?" and all the things we miss out on as individuals and as a family because we have two children with special needs. There are missed opportunities, missed friendships, strained family relationships, misunderstandings of our motives or our reasoning for not accepting invitations to do things, why we have germ phobia, etc. These are all part of the sacrifices we have to make with special needs children in our family.

I am not going to follow the path of whining. We as a family have been "wrecked" in a different sense of the word. We have been wrecked in a beautiful, remarkable way. I had the pleasure of reviewing and helping launch a book by a fellow author. It's called *Wrecked*, by Jeff Goins, and it's a journey of "unbecoming," covering the stories of people whose lives have been turned upside-down in the best way possible—and what they decided to do afterward.

Jeff explained it in the following description of his book:

> *We all want to know why were put on this earth, why we were created. But the answer may, in fact, shock you. Whether it's a trip to the developing world, a brush with poverty, or a painful tragedy, we all need moments that change the way we see the world, moments that challenge our complacency and call us to something more.*
>
> *Once you've been wrecked, there's no going back. And perhaps that's not such a bad thing.*

When Matthew came into our lives, with no warning of how things would be different and how our life path would change forever, we were on a path to a life of mediocrity, complacency and being comfortable. We were Christians; attended church regularly, taught Sunday school, talked about God often and even did some missionary work. But we weren't wrecked. And now, as our family has grown to a family of seven with the addition of Isaac, God has chosen to wreck us once again. He is taking us to a deeper level of total reliance on Him for strength, support and healing. As our faith ebbs and flows with each new challenge and victory, as we struggle to keep our eyes on what God is doing in the bigger picture and how we are to use our experiences to further glorify Him, we are being wrecked.

What does being wrecked look like from our perspective? Wrecked means a life measured by each breath taken and each beat of the heart for each of our children, special needs or not. Wrecked means choosing to believe that God is in control and He has blessed us as a family with a way to be able to see Him and His fingerprints in our lives with more clarity and frequency than most people. Being wrecked looks like we have everything under control on the front side with smiles and composure, but on the back side we fall to our knees, even prone on our face crying out to God for even just a little strength to get through the next day. Being wrecked comes from knowing that crying out to anyone other than God is just crying and whining. Wrecked is being available to share what God is doing in our lives and through all five of our children, for Him to be glorified and praised, even when we are at the end of our strength and just want rest. Wrecked means being vulnerable, misunderstood, misquoted...all the while knowing God sees what is in our heart, our minds and our motives when dealing with family, friends and anyone else who has never been wrecked. The process of being wrecked has made each of us more compassionate, more tolerant, more patient, has us praying more and has made our faith simpler by being completely reliant on God. Being wrecked is holding your ten-week-old baby in a quiet hospital room, staring eye to eye for nearly an hour straight…a gaze which would melt the heart of even the hardest of souls in need of being wrecked.

> *This is what anyone who has been wrecked can hope for: to be led where you once didn't want to go and actually be glad you get there. It means to have a transformation that goes beyond mere words—to be introduced to another way of life, to follow in the footsteps of a teacher who is calling you through the eye of a needle. Often it involves being catalyzed by an encounter with pain. The process is horrible and ugly and completely gut-wrenching—and at the same time, beautiful. It is real and hard and true. Most of all, it is necessary.* **Wrecked: When a Broken Word Slams Into Your Comfortable Life, by Jeff Goins**

What is your wrecked experience? Are you in need of being wrecked? I know I am. "The process is horrible and ugly and completely gut-wrenching—

and at the same time, beautiful." As our God continues to wreck our family, I pray that you are also wrecked…in a beautiful and remarkable way.

Prayer: *Lord, help me be wrecked in a beautiful way. I understand the process can be painful and gut wrenching at times…but it can also be beautiful. Help me to convey to other people what being wrecked truly is. I pray for those who have never been wrecked in a way that transforms them and takes them into a deeper relationship with you. I thank you for wrecking my life and taking me out of a life of complacency. Amen.*

From the Inside Out

THE SAYING "FROM the inside out" has many different meanings attached to it. The band Hillsong United, on their *Live in Miami* album, has a song by this title which is sung in churches small and large all around the world. We lived this song and the lyrics as we tended to and sat with our new little Isaac.

Matthew gave us a trial run on this as he fulfilled his desire to go from the inside of his room to the outside. Rather than use his doorknob—the easier solution—he had to find a more challenging way to do the mundane task of opening the door and exiting his room. He picked away at the bottom corner of the door until he found a weak spot, and from there it was downhill. Piece by piece, he picked away at the wood, chipping off small, medium and large portions that he threw to the side as he neared his goal. This was all done in the wee hours of the morning while the rest of us were sleeping. When we finally did hear him, he was already through the first layer and making his way to the second layer of the door.
There are different views when you look from the inside out and then from the outside in. When Isaac was born, there were times when we were stuck in

the cycle of hospital, emotional breakdowns, spiritual highs and lows, grace, peace, fear, a needed hug, hope, some sleep, worry. This cycle represents the ups and downs of what life looks like when weeks go by without a clear picture of when we may go home from a stay in the hospital. All our strength and emotion was centered on Isaac and the rest of our family as we tried to hold our lives together. To be completely honest, it was a test of faith and strength. I cannot completely share in words how hard it was to see our precious little one suffer. How hard it was to see and hear Theresa cry out to God to make it all stop and go away. Sure, from the outside looking in, it may appear that we can hold it together, but what you don't see is me sitting in the middle of a lake, alone in my fishing boat crying out to God. What you don't see is Theresa in the car, crying and asking when it's all going to end.

We'd been in these situations before, dealing with surgeries, procedures, suctioning, medications, treatments, therapies, etc. We'd experienced the ups and the downs many times. But there are times and places where God was doing a mighty work, transforming us, cleansing us, breaking us down and changing our family from the inside out. We were forced, with permission, to be consumed from the inside out. No false front, no mask, no facade of "everything is fine." This is when we moved from doing things with our own strength and stamina to completely surrendering and falling into the Father's arms. We stumbled and fell, we got up and stumbled again, but eventually we reached the spot where we allowed ourselves to be caught in His embrace. These are some of the lyrics to a song which had both of us in tears. As we listened to it, we both felt as though it was more than a worship song meant for a congregation; it was meant to be sung from our hearts as the battle armor fell off one piece at a time.

A thousand times I've failed
Still Your mercy remains
And should I stumble again
Still I'm caught in Your grace
Everlasting, Your light will shine when all else
fades
Never ending, Your glory goes beyond all fame
Your will above all else
My purpose remains
The art of losing myself
In bringing You praise
Everlasting, Your light will shine when all else
fades
Never ending, Your glory goes beyond all fame

My heart and my soul
I give You control
Consume me from the inside out, Lord
Let justice and praise
Become my embrace
To love you from the inside out.
Hillsong United, Live In Miami album

As we are transformed from the inside out, God shows up in unexpected ways. Isaac, with no words spoken, no gospel preached, no action even taken, is proclaiming the power of God loud and clear. God opens doors and allows people to see from the outside in as we are being transformed and wearing our faith and our actions on our sleeves. We pray in that in the art of losing ourselves, God will be praised and bring us opportunities to share Him with others. Total reliance on God is not easy and not predictable, whether it means a spiritual lift, an emotional lift or even a financial lift when it's needed the most.

I won't sugar coat the reality of what is needed for Isaac, as well as for the rest of the Troupe family. Isaac has had rough weeks. Our family as a whole has had rough weeks; weeks which include many different days of surgeries and procedures. There may be more in the future due to other complications from those procedures and surgeries; times when our immediate prayer is focused on healing and praying against infections of the various sites around his body where there are holes one normally does not have. For example, Isaac has a tracheostomy to assist with his breathing, a new feeding tube placed in his belly and a new, more permanent line to replace a regular style IV which needs to move every few days. I counted almost 20 pokes from head to toe as they tried to find a new line site...which resulted in a newly shaved area on his head as well as bruises at every spot of attempt. There have been times when he was on the ventilator and kept mildly sedated to allow him to rest and heal. These are times when we need prayer because these things leave us realizing how difficult it is to look to the future and wondering how we will be able to endure what is ahead, both in the hospital and at home.

If you were wondering what happened to the door...in true *Monsters, Inc.* fashion (you need to see the movie) I glued every piece back together, then skinned the affected areas with a thin plywood. We had to salvage the door. Why, you ask? Because on the side facing the hallway, we have pencil marks with dates that show the heights of each of our children from the time we moved into the house in 1999 to today; it is priceless.

Prayer: *Father, help me be transformed from the inside out. When I am consumed with all that is happening around me, help me to see that you are there, and help me to praise you as I am being changed. Your light does shine when all else is fading...let me not lose sight of that light. Amen.*

Tragedy, Then Trust

As Jairus and Jesus were going to Jairus's home a messenger arrived from the home of Jairus, the leader of the synagogue. He told him, "Your daughter is dead. There's no use troubling the Teacher now." But when Jesus heard what had happened, he said to Jairus, "Don't be afraid. Just have faith, and she will be healed" (Luke 8:49–50 NLT). Jairus was whipsawed between the contrasting messages. The first, from the servants: "Your daughter is dead." The second, from Jesus: "Don't be afraid." Horror called from one side. Hope compelled from the other. Tragedy, then trust. Jairus heard two voices and had to choose which one he would heed. Don't we all? **Fearless: Imagine Your Life Without Fear, by Max Lucado**

I COULDN'T AGREE more with Max Lucado in this snapshot of trust. Being "whipsawed between the two contrasting messages" Is a great description of the events we experienced when Isaac was born in the early morning hours of May 6; we whipsawed back and forth between messages like, "You are having a baby today!" "Airlift to Ann Arbor, mom and baby or just baby?" "Will there be an airway to work with?" "Surgery may be necessary immediately." All of these contrasted with the same calming words Jesus spoke to Jairus. "Don't be afraid." All the plans we made, all of the little details of what June 8 would look like and the following weeks of care, family planning, dog sitting, school and other commitments were shoved to the side as we were thrust into this situation of complete reliance on God, those around us, our family and our church family.

We had accepted the fact Isaac would not be perfect in the eyes of this world, but perfect in God's eyes and ours. We had accepted he would probably share some of the same issues as Matthew and even produce some of his own. We had embraced and were galvanized in our resolve to take on the challenge of another CHARGE child. What we were not prepared for was not doing it on our terms. In an instant, we were back and forth between tragedy and trust. Just as Jairus was presented two voices—one of horror and one of hope—we heard two voices; we had to choose which one we would heed.

Many may never know the great impact of the prayers of our church family has had on our family; they prayed Isaac into this world during the church services that morning, and they prayed him through surgery when he was just a few days old as well. They prayed not just for Isaac, but for mom, dad and family too. We experienced the support offered by 7,000 page views on our blog site *Lessons from Matthew & Isaac*, and felt the prayers of thousands of people at our home church and other churches around our city and beyond that Sunday morning. We can truly say Isaac is not our own...he belongs to God—a product of faith and answered prayer. Tragedy, then trust.

Prayer: *Lord, be my constant focus when I am being pulled in two different directions when in the middle of a crisis. Help me to see that you are bigger than any crisis could be. When I hear two conflicting messages, draw me to your truth no matter how convincing the bad news sounds. Help me to embrace your calming words; "Do not be afraid." Amen.*

Sunshine above the Clouds

The disciples fought the storm for nine cold, skin drenching hours. And about 4:00 a.m. the unspeakable happened. They spotted someone coming on the water. "A ghost!" they said, crying out in terror. (Matthew 14:26 MSG). They didn't expect Jesus to come to them this way. Neither do we. We expect him to come in the form of peaceful hymns or Easter Sundays or quiet retreats. We expect to find Jesus in morning devotionals, church suppers, and meditation. We never expect to see him in a bear market, pink slip, lawsuit, foreclosure, or war. We never expect to see him in a storm. But it is in storms that he does his finest work, for it is in storms that he has our keenest attention. **Fearless: Imagine Your Life Without Fear, by Max Lucado**

PICTURE THE WEATHER people during a storm who are covered in all-weather gear, waves crashing in the background, barely able to stand with the whipping wind making the traffic signs wave back and forth. Yeah, this is kind of where I have found myself. This early journey with Isaac has been scary and wonderful all at the same time. It's like marveling at the wonder of nature as a thunderstorm rolls in, wreaks its havoc, moves on and leaves a beautiful sunset behind. We have had days that end with a beautiful sunset as well as days that end with thunder still in the distance, all the while hoping and praying the phone doesn't ring with the delivery of bad news or another flash of lightning.

As Peter took his step of faith, as Jesus asked him to do, he was fine as long as his gaze was upon Jesus. I find myself there too. One of the hardest things I had to do as Isaac's hospital stay turned from days into weeks and then into months was to pull Theresa away and take her home at night. Theresa was being torn between comforting, holding and just being there for every one of Isaac's cries; tending to Sarah Anne, who just wanted to know if baby Isaac would be okay; being with Matthew, who just wanted her to stay home; and tending to her own healing from her C-section surgery. It's times like these when your gaze comes off the outstretched hand of a waiting Lord and begin to sink, become weak in your faith and take your eyes off the bigger work God is doing. You begin to think about nurses and wonder if they check on your baby enough and comfort them the same way you would. You wonder if you'll miss a doctor's update or a change in care. But you just have to drive home and trust. Trust that the Son is above the clouds of this current storm.

> *His call to courage is not a call to naiveté or ignorance. We aren't oblivious to the overwhelming challenges that life brings. We're to counterbalance them with long looks at God's accomplishments. "We must pay much closer attention to what we have heard, so that we do not drift away from it" Heb. 2:1 (NASB). Do whatever it takes to keep your gaze on Jesus.*
> ***Fearless: Imagine Your Life Without Fear, by Max Lucado***

This quote is a call to courage, a call for me to keep my eyes upon the Healer as He heals through the doctors and caregivers at the hospital. It's a call to keep my eyes on what God has already done in Isaac's short life, and to keep my eyes on all of the miracles I've seen and the work He has done in Matthew's life and in the rest of our family.

Prayer: Jesus, as you reach out your stretched hand, may I have the courage to reach for it and step out of the boat during the storms in my life. Help me to keep my eyes fixed on yours and not to focus on the crashing waves, the flashing lightning and the roar of thunder around me. Only you have the power to silence the storms in my life. Help me to remember that you are not just present at a retreat, at church or in my personal prayer time, but that you are there beside me when the clouds begin to roll in. Amen.

Lush Grass or Cold Rocky Crags?

LUSH GRASS, FERTILE soil, butterflies, meadow flowers, fragrant pines, soft ferns, a beautiful babbling brook; a valley has all the makings of a perfect postcard picture. So, why do so many of us long for a mountaintop experience?

I finished a great book recently by Andy Andrews titled, *The Noticer: Sometimes, All a Person Needs is a Little Perspective*. It's a casual story about a man who mysteriously shows up in people's lives at an opportune time and helps them find "a little perspective" in the situations in which they find themselves. It was the perfect read for the journey my family and I are on and how this new leg of our journey became a much larger expedition for our family.

Theresa and I found ourselves expecting a new addition; a second son who was set to arrive at the end of May 2013. Without going into all of the details, there was substantial enough information in the different ultrasounds and fetal echocardiogram to determine he was likely to join Matthew in the CHARGE Syndrome corner. The puzzle was coming together to form a familiar pattern and picture. Nothing was certain, but we had to assemble the "team" that would be present at his birth.

Theresa and I knew our new baby boy would enter this world with challenges similar to the ones we experienced with Matthew. What we did not know until the day arrived was the extent and severity of the challenges.

Theresa and I don't dwell on asking God the "why" question, but more the "how" question. "How are how do we take on this new challenge?" We know strength will come, but it can be hard when you are in the infancy of processing bad news.

I mentioned Andy's book earlier, and here are some of the words he wrote:

Everybody wants to be on the mountaintop, but if you'll remember, mountaintops are rocky and cold. There is not growth on the top of a mountain. Sure, the view is great, but what's a view for? A view just gives us a glimpse of our next destination—our next target. But to hit that target, we must come off the mountain, go through the valley, and begin to climb the next slope. It is in the valley that we slog through the lush grass and rich soil, learning and becoming what enables us to summit life's next peak. **The Noticer: Sometimes, All a Person Needs is a Little Perspective**

We had to try on new hiking shoes, test and size up new walking sticks, select gear and outfit our packs; we had the next summit in view and get ready for the expedition of our lives. It is not easy leaving the comfort of the valley to head up the mountain of whatever journey God is about to take us on. One thing I am confident of is that each journey He has planned will also challenge us and will continue to shape our character and our identity in Him. For each of our journeys up the mountain you could choose no better outfitter and guide than our creator.

Prayer: *Lord, thank you for the mountaintop experiences I have had where I feel closer to you than ever before. When it is time to come down and begin the dangerous trek down the mountainside and journey through the valley, help me keep my perspective. It is only through journeying through the valleys that I can reach the next mountain. Help me to feel enriched and energized as much in the valley as I do on the mountain. Amen.*

Can Lightning Strike Twice? Please Pray, It May Have

ACCORDING TO THE NOAA (National Oceanic and Atmospheric Administration), the odds of getting struck by lightning in one's lifetime is 1:10,000. One would have better odds of this phenomenon happening than to have a child born with CHARGE Syndrome (1:12,000).

Then, one day we had the usual monthly appointment with the OB/GYN when Theresa was at 22 weeks gestation with Isaac. I will let her; in her own words describe the morning:

> *...While I was showering and getting ready, I was thinking about the day ahead and the much-anticipated ultrasound to hopefully find out the baby's gender. As I was thinking about the baby, I was overwhelmed with the thought of how THIS baby was meticulously created by God for our family, down to each hair (or lack thereof) on its head. Whether a boy or girl, this baby was what God planned for our family and would be the best.*

Even though the news received just moments after being told "it's a boy!" was shocking, and not what we were expecting, I think we were better prepared than most to receive it. We have been walking this "special" road for almost 11 years together already. Knowing Kevin, my rock, was sitting next to me and would continue to hold my hand through this next portion of our walk was my encouragement…not that it could stop the flow of my tears.

Hearing the news our baby was going to be physically not as perfect as we hoped, I was still quite emotional as we stopped at the scheduling desk to discuss our next appointment (a planned fetal echocardiogram, as is custom after having a child with known heart conditions). I know it was no coincidence the scheduler's radio was playing one of my favorite songs, which I think God used to continue to comfort me. The song was "Your Grace is Enough" by Chris Tomlin. It was the best song for me to hear at that moment!

Theresa and I have become pretty good at reading ultrasounds, MRIs, fetal echoes and all kinds of other charts and tests. We could tell there was something not quite right with our little boy's face—a cleft. The technician tried to glaze over it, but as Theresa stated the obvious, the technician went to get Theresa's doctor to confirm what she saw.

Now, a cleft is actually a very common birth defect and can usually be just an isolated event, but, we could not rule out the possibility that it was CHARGE related. We had seen lightning strike before—with Matthew—but could not believe that lightning might strike twice. The statistical chances of the same parents having a second child with CHARGE Syndrome are between one and two percent. Twenty to thirty percent of all CHARGE Syndrome births have a cleft lip, cleft palate or both. We believe God DOES NOT deal in statistics!

> *For you created my inmost being; you knit me together in my mother's womb. I praise you because I am fearfully and wonderfully made; your works are wonderful, I know that full well.*
> **Psalm 139:13–14**

Needless to say, we experienced a flood of different emotions over those few days. We were excited about having another boy yet shocked over the realization we could be walking a familiar path. The difference with Matthew, though, was that we were completely reactive and had no prior knowledge of what we were about to experience in the CHARGE syndrome journey. With Isaac, we had to wait and see if he would and how he would be affected over the next several months, as pieces were revealed to us through various tests and procedures. Either way, together we were prepared to await his arrival. Honestly, the waiting was not easy. With Matthew in our lives we know first-hand the challenges that could come our way. One thing that was a constant was that Theresa and I were bonded in our resolve that this child (Isaac) was the one that God had chosen and planned for us from the beginning of time.

Prayer: *Father, thank you for creating each one of us unique a special in your eyes. You knit me together in my mother's womb exactly the way you wanted me and I know I am perfect in your eyes. I take comfort knowing that I am fearfully and wonderfully made, as are each one of my children. You are not a God of imperfection and not a God who would make a mistake. Help me to embrace the ones I have been entrusted with and give me the strength to care for them well. Your grace is enough for me. Amen.*

If You Pray For a Beach, Expect Sand

TEST RESULTS OF Matthew's visit to the endocrinologist show that after a three-year period of no weight gain and no growth, Matthew gained six pounds and grew an inch since his heart surgery to repair a leaking mitral valve. This was a remarkable surge in a good direction for Matthew's overall health. We could not have planned this out come any better. In fact, we had nothing to do with this plan...ours was completely different based on the information we had and the choices given to us at first.

As I was preparing to write this chapter I had many things which were swimming around in my head...as is often the case, something happened which caught my attention and wrangled my thoughts in the direction of this topic. I can thank a friend who posted this on a Facebook post:

> *"Praying, not intervening...this one is probably one of the hardest for me to remember."* **Debby Albrecht**

Thanks Debby, I needed to hear this. My prayer life has been completely opposite of praying, expecting God to act and accepting what the outcome is, whatever it may be. Without realizing it, I believe my prayer had been telling God about the situation (as if He didn't know of it already) then trying to manipulate events, interjecting my own ideas and theories on how the situation needed to be resolved, then wondering why things didn't go according to my plan. As a reminder I had to go back to the basics; how it is supposed to be done; Jesus taught us how to pray as He taught His disciples:

> *So I say to you: Ask and it will be given to you; seek and you will find; knock and the door will be opened to you. For everyone who asks receives; the one who seeks finds; and to the one who knocks, the door will be opened.* **Luke 11:9–10**

Back to the prayer for Matthew and the surgery to repair his leaking mitral valve. Our prayer from the beginning was for God to heal him. We were faced with many options and some of those options changed over time. Our prayer of healing remained constant. Early choices were replacement of his heart valve and another was a replacement with a mechanical valve. God had other plans for this situation. We dwelled on the two options and weighed the pros and the cons of only the two solutions. As time passed Matthew grew and the doctors were able to see something from the tests that could not be seen before. Matthew had a cleft in the valve flap that provided a third choice that proved to be less invasive, less risky and a more permanent solution.

Seems so simple, doesn't it? Try it; it's not that easy. As I have heard before, and have reminded myself over and over, God answers prayer in three ways: yes, no and not yet. The first two may be abrupt and hard to swallow, but the latter is the tougher one. Having to wait on His timing, especially the longer the time period, opens up further opportunity for Him to intervene.

As we prayed through this situation we prayed for a beautiful beach, complete with white-capped waves, bright blue skies and a gentle breeze. We got the beach but also learned that a beach is made of countless grains of sand. Each prayer offered, every option given and each turn of events is a grain of sand. Each has a story, each one has been tossed by waves and blown by wind until it has become part of our beach.

Prayer: *Father, I know your plan is perfect. Give me the patience to wait on you and the ability to resist the temptation to manipulate the outcome. Help me not to confuse a length of time as abandonment from you. I am grateful that when I knock, you answer. Help me see each grain of sand as it becomes a part of my beach. Amen.*

The Holy City

TWO WEEKS INTO a three-week journey, I found myself looking out a hotel room window at the city of Jerusalem. My journey took me from the Southern region of Europe in Greece to Crete, Turkey, Cypress and then on to Israel. I knew I would not be fully able to digest everything I saw and experienced until I returned home and let it all sink in. I visited the places Paul visited during the early stages of the church, walked in the footsteps of Jesus in the cities of Bethlehem, Nazareth, Galilee and Jerusalem. I stood and prayed at the place where Jesus started His public ministry, gave us the Beatitudes, ate the Last Supper, prayed His last night, and where He was crucified, left to die and buried.

What I want to share with you is the thought that occurred to me as our tour group was taking a boat ride on the Sea of Galilee; which was where Jesus approached four fishermen.

As Jesus was walking beside the Sea of Galilee, he saw two brothers, Simon called Peter and his brother Andrew. They were casting a net into the lake, for they were fishermen. "Come, follow

me," Jesus said, "and I will send you out to fish for people." At once they left their nets and followed him.
Matthew 4:18–20

In the middle of the lake, the captain shut off the motor and we sat in silence for a time to take in the moment. As I looked over the railing, I silently watched the wake of the boat as it slowed and gently drifted away from the boat. The wake went farther than my eye could see and gently merged with other ripples and waves. It occurred to me that our lives are, in many ways, like the wake of the boat. All of the words we speak and the actions we take fan out from us and spread to make a wider and wider path. The calling of the first of the twelve apostles began a wake which spread the Gospel into the world where we still see and hear of it today.

A quick glance at a dictionary gave me several meanings of the word "wake." One of which was the definition of the wake I watched drift from the boat. Another which caught my attention was this:

Verb, waked or woke, waked or wok•en, wak•ing, noun
–verb (used without object)

98

1. To become roused from sleep; awake; awaken; waken (often fol. by up).
2. To become roused from a tranquil or inactive state; awaken; waken: to wake from one's daydreams.
3. To become cognizant or aware of something; awaken; waken: to wake to the true situation.

As I watched the wake of the boat, this definition came into focus a little more. I believe we can all get a little complacent and stagnant in our lives. By being in this place, the Holy Land of Israel, I was "awakened" again.

Though my life and my circumstances can sometimes bog me down, I don't believe for a second Matthew was given to Theresa and me by pure chance. I wept when I had a chance to have a video conference with my family and Matthew signed "Dad" as well as "I love you" when he saw me on the computer. Theresa told me that while I was gone, Sarah Anne walked by the computer at home and said "hi" to it on the off chance I might be there. I missed Hannah and Megan and could not wait to share with them a renewed and alive Bible experience. And mostly, I looked forward to holding my wife, so I could wish her a happy wedding anniversary in person after being separated on our special day.

Prayer: *Lord, thank you for the opportunities you create in my life to be awakened. May my actions, my words and my deeds flow out and become wider and wider as they further affect those I come into contact with. My desire is to fill that wake with words and actions that reflect you. Amen.*

Know Where You Are

THE PLACE WHERE I take my annual retreat and fishing trip is a beautiful 7,000-acre piece of property in northern lower Michigan. Several lakes and nearly 60 miles of two-track roads crisscross the land. One afternoon while it was rainy and windy, a few of my fellow fishermen decided to search out one of the smaller lakes that are only accessible by trekking through the woods. We did find a lake, but we also got lost in the process. It was an adventure with no map to go by, but we were reassured by the fact that there were borders on the property, so even on 7,000 acres one could not stay lost for long. After about an hour and a beautiful view of a part of the property we'd never seen before, we made it back to camp.

In a 1917 Popular Mechanics magazine advertisement for a Leedawl Dollar Compass the ad copy reads; "You need more than your eyes to read a map–the best ever drawn is useless, unless you know direction". This is so very true in many aspects of life. We have to know where we are and what direction we are facing if we have any chance at getting where we want to go in life. It requires an honest, real "gut check" of where we are currently and in what direction we are heading in our relationships with our spouse and kids, our finances and especially our walk with God.

I am convinced it usually takes some kind of tragedy or difficult circumstance to bring us back to the reality and fragility of life. Crisis situations are a true test of where we are, both physically and spiritually. It is also a true measure of the quality and commitment of the people you spend time with and who you call "friends."

We had our own reality check which tested our training and response when Theresa was putting Sarah Anne to bed one night while I was unloading the dishwasher in the kitchen just about twenty feet from Isaac's bed. For the first three years of his life, Isaac resided in our great room so he was always close to the pulse of our home. As I was working, I heard a change in Isaac's breathing so I quickly turned around and started toward him. As I got closer, I saw that he was pulling hard at his oxygen tubing and HME (his artificial nose, which is attached to the end of his trachea tube). In all his tugging and playing, he had pulled his trachea tube out of his throat, leaving him gasping for air and turning blue. I screamed for Theresa's help and within seconds we were able to get a new one in place and his airway open again. This event was a definite reality check, and another reminder that we cannot take even the smallest break from being on-call to Isaac's needs. Our response was so quick, his low oxygen sensor alarm was just sounding as we finished. The first alarm was his heart rate, and I am sure if we were wearing a heart monitor ours would have been going off as well!

Always be ready, never become complacent, do not waiver.

But make sure that you don't get so absorbed and exhausted in taking care of all your day-by-day obligations that you lose track of the time and doze off, oblivious to God. The night is about over, dawn is about to break. Be up and awake to what God is doing! God is putting the finishing touches on the salvation work he began when we first believed. We can't afford to waste a minute, must not squander these precious daylight hours in frivolity and indulgence, in sleeping around and dissipation, in bickering and grabbing everything in sight. Get out of bed and get dressed! Don't loiter and linger, waiting until the very last minute. Dress yourselves in Christ, and be up and about! **Romans 13:11–14 (MSG)**

Where are you right now? What direction are you facing? I don't mean your physical location. I am talking about your spiritual walk. The most elaborate map (or plan) in the world is useless unless you know where you are and where you are heading.

Many people wonder how we deal with the ups and downs of medically fragile children. My answer is we don't deal with it alone. We lean on each other. We lean on those we may not know personally, but know as a fellow traveler on the same road. We lean on our faith in a God who made each one of us unique and perfect in His eyes. We also accept these children are not our own. They belong to a larger family of people who pray for us and support us. We deal with it by being transparent and allowing our experiences to be used to share our story with others who are hurting or have, as the words above say, lost track of time and dozed off. We are encouraged by encouraging others.

Prayer: *Lord, thank you for being my map. Help me not to become complacent in my responsibilities in caring for my family, fulfilling the ministry you have given me or in my relationship with you. Remind and* *direct me when I begin to lose my way. Show me ways to be vigilant in knowing where I am and give me the strength and courage to make changes when a course redirect is needed. I choose you to be my map maker. Give me wisdom to be able to read the map consistently, accurately and with confidence. Amen.*

Do You Care?

I LOVE BOOKS and the stories people share of their personal journeys. One recent book I finished was written by Ian Brown called *The Boy in the Moon*. Ian is the father of a boy with a rare genetic disorder, not unlike the one Matthew and Isaac have. As I read his book, I resonated with many of the feelings and situations Ian expressed and experienced. I felt a certain kinship as I scanned the pages and compared the stories he shared of caring for his son, both good ones of victories and milestones, and the not so good ones of staying up all night, cleaning poo and not being able to communicate.

He made a reference to a system they had for storing the educational toys they'd been offered from local agencies and therapists to help with his son's developmental delays. He recalled a moment when he peered at the label on one of the toys. It had the name of the agency it was from with an address to return the toy in the event it was no longer needed. It was a defeated moment. His child may never "get it." We have had those moments too. Cabinets filled with hope, but no interest from Matthew or Isaac.

Theresa and I can easily get overwhelmed with feelings of defeat when we're beaten down with sleep deprivation, around the clock medical care for Isaac and having to constantly watch Matthew so he doesn't harm himself, someone else or property. We sometimes get exasperated by health care bureaucracy and systems that seem to hire people who are completely unaware of the people on the other end of their decisions and actions. There seem to be endless medications, feedings, diapers, doctor appointments, therapy and did I mention sleep deprivation?

This is what it is like to have no hope. This is what it is like if you look at this journey as just having a child with a disability, a genetic mutation; a freak of nature.

> *"For I know the plans I have for you," declares the LORD, "plans to prosper you and not to harm you, plans to give you hope and a future. Then you will call on me and come and pray to me, and I will listen to you. You will seek me and find me when you seek me with all your heart."* ***Jeremiah 29:11–13***

For whatever reason, God chose Theresa and me to take care of Matthew and Isaac. He knows the plans He has for us. It is a perfect plan made just for us, so what we need to do is pray and seek Him with all of our heart. Some say we have been gifted to take care of them, others say we have been given more patience. I believe that everyone has been gifted with the ability to care. In some people, this gift is very apparent. Others just need something or someone to care about.

Here is an interesting quote from author, blogger and marketing guru Seth Godin. It deals more in the lines of the business world but I think you will see how it can be applicable to many situations.

> *No organization cares about you. Organizations aren't capable of this. Your bank, certainly, doesn't care. Neither does your HMO or even your car dealer. It's amazing to me that people are surprised to discover this fact.*

> *People, on the other hand, are perfectly capable of caring. It's part of being a human. It's only when organizational demands and regulations get in the way that the caring fades.*

If you want to build a caring organization, you need to fill it with caring people and then get out of their way. When your organization punishes people for caring, don't be surprised when people stop caring. When you free your employees to act like people (as opposed to cogs in a profit-maximizing efficient machine) then the caring can't help but happen. **Seth Godin**

We have had experiences on both sides of the caring coin. On the ugly side, we were told by a medical professional that Matthew would never have survived before modern medicine and that it was the way nature weeded out the weak. That was uplifting. We have also been told not to expect too much and not to set the bar too high or we will just be disappointed. More than once we have received evil looking stares while trying to comfort Matthew when he is upset and we cannot interpret his want or need. Several times we've gotten dirty looks when Matthew is just making "happy" noises. We've listened to whispering and giggling after we pass people who apparently find a little boy in a wheelchair making noises as funny and an opportunity for ridicule. Although Isaac is a bright and happy baby boy, he has scars from cleft surgery and he still has a trachea tube to breathe, which brings on yet another round of stares and whispers.

On the amazing side of caring, we have been hugged and supported by strangers. There have been doctors who have prayed with us and who have witnessed miracles alongside us. We have had people bless us financially when they had no idea we were struggling and times when food has been dropped on our doorstep. We have experienced people caring for us with just a kind word and letters, cards and uplifting comments on my blog. People have reached out and helped us travel to a needed conference or doctor's appointments and given rides across the state so our girls could attend events and have some "normal" time as we cared for our boys in the hospital. Total strangers have blessed us at Christmastime while we were out of state for a month during the holidays for treatment. And, most of all, people pray for us regularly and seek God with their whole heart on our behalf.

I am going to ask you the question I need to ask myself many times when things get tough and my instinct is to do the wrong thing; what side of caring are you on?

Prayer: *Lord, give me the strength to care. As people, caregivers and doctors pass through our lives, allow me to be a shining light. When I'm troubled by someone who seemingly does not care, allow me to reflect on the fact that you care. I thank you for the ways you care for me directly and through those you have placed around me. Amen.*

Wounds or Scars?

I REMEMBER MAY 1, 2011 very well. It was exactly one month since Matthew had his open heart surgery to repair his leaking mitral valve. Interestingly, it was only in the previous week or so Matthew allowed us to raise his shirt and look at his chest surgery scar. He even posed for a few pictures. The wound or incision had almost completely healed, even though his breastplate was not completely fused at the time.

Of course, I was always looking for things I could write about, so I started to ponder why Matthew didn't want us to look at his wound, but willingly allowed us to look at his scar. Apart from the obvious reason of it being painful, why was he so hesitant to let us look at the wound?

> *There is something beautiful about all scars of whatever nature. A scar means the hurt is over, the wound is closed and healed, done with.*
> **Harry Crews**

I started to recall the many scars on my body. As a carpenter, I have many of them on my hands, some on my arms, some on my legs and even a few on my head. Each one has a story that goes with it. Some of them I am not too proud of, as they were the result of doing something stupid, like shooting a finishing nail through my finger with a nail gun or using a utility knife the wrong way. Matthew has a few scars that are the result of carelessness or simply an unfortunate accident. I can count seven larger scars on Matthew's frame which were intentional, a result of decisions we made for him in the form of surgeries we put him through to make his life better and more comfortable and to prevent further pain.

As I write this, we are a week past Easter; a time when we reflect on the death and resurrection of Jesus, on the sacrifices He made for us at the cross, the pain and suffering that were the result of a single act of love for us.

> *But he was pierced for our transgressions, he was crushed for our iniquities; the punishment that brought us peace was on him, and by his wounds we are healed.* **Isaiah 53:5**

Don't read too deeply into this statement, but I was struck by the fact that Jesus now shows the scars of seven distinct wounds—one on each hand, one on each foot, one from a pierced side, some on his head from the crown of thorns and some on his back from the leather strap or reed when he was scourged. All of these wounds were intentional and for our benefit, to make our life better, more comfortable and to prevent further pain for us.

Thomas was not with the other apostles when Jesus first appeared to them after He rose from the dead. Thomas was not going to believe until he was able to place his fingers in the wounds on Jesus' hands and side. I think many may say, or have said, how silly Thomas' comments were. The other apostles had already seen the risen Lord. Wasn't their witness enough?

I can say with certainty that we prayed and thought long and hard about each surgery and procedure that would leave a wound; we intentionally made those decisions for Matthew. God has done the same for you and for me. There are wounds which have been healed in my life as the result of the suffering His Son endured for me on the cross. Like Matthew, when they were still wounds it was hard for me to let people see and touch them. But, now they are scars with which I can proudly witness the power of healing and allow the story to be shared.

115

Do you have wounds which you just won't let go of and let heal? Begin today to turn them into scars.

Prayer: Lord, I am thankful for the scars in my life. Each one tells a story of how you healed an open wound. I pray for those who have hurt me and caused those wounds. I ask for you to heal their wounds as you have healed mine. Jesus, I am thankful for the wounds you endured and for the scars you have that remind me of your love for me. Give me the strength to allow you to show through the scars I have, and help me celebrate with others as they tell the stories of their scars and the healing which has taken place. May I wear my scars well and not let them turn back into wounds when the healing has already taken place! Amen.

Thermometer or Thermostat?

SETH GODIN PUBLISHED a book I read called *Tribes*. It is a collection of daily blog entries over a one year period. One of the entries was titled "Thermometer or Thermostat," in which he likened the action and reaction of marketing to these two tools. Do you just record the temperature or do you make changes as needed?

There was a lot more to it than that, but it made me recall the days Theresa and I spent in the surgery and Cardiac Pediatric Intensive Care waiting rooms and how different emotions we experienced were compared to the many others who were sharing in a similar experience of a child facing cardiac surgery.

Many of the faces of the family members were those of thermometers, directly showing the ups and downs of the news which came from the operating room, recovery room and from the days their child stayed in the Intensive Care Unit. Now, Theresa and I also experienced some of those same ups and downs, but I can also say we were prepared and equipped ahead of time with a thermostat which allowed us to adjust our actions accordingly. Our thermostat consisted of thousands of people who, with a Tweet, text or Facebook update, would go to the Father with the power of many voices raised in prayer. The thermostat also contained the power of peace, knowing that whatever the outcome, we accepted it as God's plan, even to the point of handing our precious boy back into His hands. Our thermostat contained the Truth of God's Word.

God is our refuge and strength, an ever-present help in trouble. **Psalms 46:1**

We were not the only ones in the waiting room who had a thermometer equipped with a thermostat. There was another amazing family God arranged for us to meet. It was not just a chance meeting, because our paths continued to cross, even to the point of having beds next to each other in the Intensive Care Unit and sharing the same room on the regular Cardiac Pediatric floor. We were able to pray our children through recovery and rejoice with each other's families and friends as our children progressed to being discharged. We were a witness to all who entered our little room, from doctors, nurses and other patients' families who seemed to be drawn to our room as God was glorified and His community of believers grew.

118

But back to the thermometer for a moment. I felt the pain of those who did not have the power of a thermostat. I hurt for those who did not have the hope of a future beyond the words which came from the lips of a doctor or nurse. I felt the pain of a young couple whose child was air-lifted from South Dakota, another family who had been there for over a month and had two very young children at home; both families several states away from home and seemingly with no support. Even though we faced our own moments of trial, we reached out and prayed for others whose only hope was in human words and the current reading of the thermometer.

My prayer is that I won't forget the thermometer, as it is a great tool, but it is more powerful when used along with the thermostat.

Which one do you find yourself focusing on the most…thermometer or thermostat?

Prayer: Father, help me to make the adjustments to my inner thermostat by spending time in your Word and in prayer. When the temperature of the situations I find myself in makes the thermometer rise and fall, be my constant help. Draw me back to your truth that you will never forsake or abandon me. Help me to be a thermostat that calms the "thermometer" people in my life. Teach me to use both in the way you want me to use them. Amen.

The Pain Passes

MY FAMILY HAS had weeks that were difficult and weeks that were not. I remember a week that was one of the most trying for us as a family. Over a period of ten days, all six of us got the flu to some degree, whether mild or strong. We even had to cancel a trip to the University of Michigan for some pre-testing for Matthew's heart surgery. I have to note that Matthew was the quickest to rebound and become himself again. He even had a brief moment of what we like to call "obnoxiously happy," where he runs up and down our hallway flapping his arms, shrieking and laughing along the way.

I think I speak for all parents when I say how amazing it is when a glassy-eyed, fever rich child— with "fever breath" as Theresa calls it (must be a mom thing)—goes from these symptoms to up and playing with just a little fever reducer in about an hour. We have noticed with Matthew how sometimes he has even worked through the pain and still played after a surgery or immediately after a procedure.

French painter Auguste Renoir, in the final 14 years of his life, battled crippling arthritis. For the last ten years of his life, he was good friends with Henri Matisse, another artist who was nearly 28 years younger and visited him every day. The arthritis in Renoir's hands was so crippling and painful he could not pick up a brush on his own. Only after someone else placed a brush in his hand was he able to move it across the canvas. One afternoon while watching Renoir struggle with immense pain, Matisse blurted out, "Auguste, why do you continue to paint when you are in such agony?" Renoir replied, "The pain passes, but the beauty remains."

Have you ever been so passionate about something that you were willing to work through the pain? I have always been drawn to those human interest stories while watching the Olympics, where they look at an athlete's life and highlight how they overcame immense obstacles and worked through the pain of tragedy and training to finally make it to the medal stand.

But what about the rest of us? Are you or I so passionate about something that we are willing to work through the pain to get results? This thought doesn't only go with sports; it can apply to our everyday lives as well.

As we approached another surgery on Matthew's heart, we worked through the pain of the decision to do it. At first, when Matthew was very young and needed a valve replacement, we were faced with two options; get it replaced with either a mechanical valve or one from a pig's heart, or do nothing. This type of surgery is very effective, but has some negatives which made the decision harder for us. A replacement meant a lifetime of drugs (blood thinners, anti-rejection meds, etc.), regular blood tests and the ever-present danger of a nasty bump that could cause bleeding we cannot see.

The pros and cons boil down to the quantity of life versus the quality of life for Matthew. The first option would, in theory, give Matthew a longer life if everything went well. It also meant he would be faced with a regime of drugs, even more doctors' visits and limited activities, all things he would simply not understand, nor tolerate well. The option of doing nothing would allow Matthew to enjoy the happy life always had, but would leave us with the pain of a shorter time with him.

I know this is heavy stuff, but it does get better. As we worked through the pain, beauty shone through. Explained only as the fingertips of God touching the situation, miraculously we were given a third option to repair the valve. As Matthew grew, the valve began to take shape and the doctors were able to see something which was not visible before. We exercised the third option of repairing the valve, and even if the repair is not perfect, it will still be his natural valve and will improve not only the quality of life but the quantity of life in the long run.

God does nothing except in response to believing prayer. **John Wesley**

Prayer: *Father, thank you for the strength to work through the pain that sometimes comes while caring for the loved ones you have placed in my life. As Auguste Renoir said, "The pain passes, but the beauty remains." I am thankful for the opportunities to see the beauty that remains. Amen.*

Sharing Matthew

FEBRUARY IS CONGENITAL Heart Defect Awareness Month and in 2011, almost exactly four years since Matthew had a cleft repair done on a leaking mitral valve, I wrote the following journal entry.

> *As I sit next to Matthew's bed, experiencing the sounds of a pediatric cardiac intensive care unit while Saturday becomes Sunday, I am overwhelmed with the goodness and faithfulness of a God who keeps His word. I am humbled by the overwhelming response of family and friends who have spread our gift of Matthew around the globe through social media and email to create an incredible chain of prayer warriors. Theresa and I are witness to the fact that prayer is powerful. We both have an undeniable trust and peace as we go through this, yet another opportunity to show God's abundant power.*
>
> *As one can imagine, on the eve of Matthew's surgery almost four years ago, I was a little restless. Something about this night was different. I can count on one hand how many*

times I have been aroused from sleep and felt the need to pray. I sat in bed and wrote the following thoughts in my journal which I believe God was using to show me He is in control of this surgery, a surgery which I believe the benefit is not just an improvement in Matthew's health; the benefit extends to all who are praying for him.

Matthew is a gift; a gift God will use to build and strengthen faith, prayer and character. Here is what I am learning...

M – Meek and humble of heart. I am learning that being meek means knowing I do not have all of the answers and knowing I have limitations. I need to rely first on God, then on those He has put around me to give support and encouragement when needed.

A – Ample supply of strength. I am learning that if I keep focused on God and continue to read and speak His truth, He will supply me with everything I need, but not necessarily everything I want. He will give me ample strength and support himself or through someone offering an encouraging word or deed.

TT – Trials and Triumph. I put the two T's together because you cannot have one without the other. One cannot taste the sweetness of triumph without first tasting the bitterness of trial. It is through trial our character is built, shaped and refined and we are able to appreciate fully the triumph in our lives.

H – Honest transparency. It is critical when dealing with heavy situations to be honest. Answering the question of, "How are you doing?" with the standard response of "I am fine" is not healthy. Many people really do want to know and it is okay to share weakness or needs. I am learning to ask for help. People really do want to help, even though they may not know what to do for me, and so they do nothing.

E – Earnest prayer. I am learning that prayer is not begging for the list of things I want or think I need. Prayer is a conversation between me and the One who knows me best and wants to bless me with everything, if only I learn His language. When I speak His language of praise, thankfulness, forgiveness, compassion and more, He reciprocates peace, understanding, faithfulness and blessings.

W – Wonder. We have a saying about Matthew: "The only predictable thing about Matthew is that he is unpredictable." God is unpredictable too, when it comes to what we think He should do. He has routinely exceeded my expectations of what I thought was right or in good portion. I am always wondering what God is going to do next to show He is God.

We still have a long time on this road of Matthew's recovery from heart surgery, both here at the hospital and continuing at home. I cannot help but see the irony that I, too, am having "heart" surgery through this experience as God continues to soften and shape my heart into one which is more like His.

It has been an amazing journey since I wrote these words in 2011. Matthew will be 14 this year! Sarah Anne will be six and Isaac has brought to us a whole set of other prayer topics. I can't stop thinking about how many times we have cried out for peace and healing and how God has handed us both in abundance over the years. I am still learning the lessons I wrote several years ago. Some of them have been bigger and broader than I ever thought possible.

Prayer: *Father, thank you for all the gifts in my life. I thank you even for the ones that bring trials because I know they will ultimately bring me triumphs. Thank you for keeping me meek and humble, for it is there that I know my strength only comes from you. Use me to be a light to others and to share you in my actions and in my words. Amen.*

He Is My Father

I REMEMBER ONE Father's Day and what began as a trip to church and an afternoon with my family lengthened and had me in constant thought of the words our pastor spoke. He echoed the words of Jesus as He spoke to his disciples just hours before He was going to be taken away from them.

> *"Do not let your hearts be troubled. You believe in God; believe also in me. My Father's house mas many rooms; if it were not so, would I have told you that I am going there to prepare a place for you? And if I go and prepare a place for you, I will come back and take you to be with me that you also may be where I am. You know the way to the place where I am going."* **John 14:1–4**

Our pastor went on to explain the preparation of our "room" in Heaven which is being prepared for us. The "room" or atmosphere which is being prepared will include all of the people we influenced on Earth. One of the experiences our pastor made a reference to was the case of a mother with a child who had special needs. He talked about the everyday struggles she endures here on earth, and you can bet he sparked my interest. He went on to explain that though the relationship involves the mom taking care of her child's needs, the relationship in Heaven will be completely different.

As Matthew had another one of his nights where 2:00 a.m. seemed to be the right time to get up for the day, I laid in bed wondering what he was laughing about. Who was talking in his ear making him laugh as if he was being torture tickled? I often think he is laughing at us; these children with special needs, I believe, are privileged to information we are not. The other thing which kept me awake was the thought of what my relationship with Matthew will be like in Heaven. He will not have vision and hearing problems, and he will be able to speak, eat and think quickly. Will he still love and accept me and want to hang out in my room with me?

I started to think beyond Matthew to my other children and beyond…my relationships, good and bad which I had in the past, currently have and will have in the future. How many people will be a part of my room? Have I had an influence on enough people to even fill the room? Will there be anybody there at all or have my relationships been nothing more than surface relationships of give and take?

In the book by the late Coach John Wooden called *A Lifetime of Observations and Reflections On and Off the Court,* he talks about some of the best advice his father gave him. After graduating from high school, his father wrote on a piece of paper his creed.

> *"Seven Things To Do"*
> *Be true to yourself.*
> *Help others.*
> *Make each day your masterpiece.*
> *Drink deeply from good books, especially the Bible.*
> *Make friendships a fine art.*
> *Build a shelter against a rainy day.*
> *Pray for guidance and count and give thanks for your blessings every day.*

What creed am I following? My prayer is to make it a point to make sure there are people in my "room" when I make it to Heaven. I think I may even adopt the above creed in my own life.

Prayer: *God, thank you for being my Father. Thank you for your guiding hand as you lead me through each of the trials in my life. As my "room" is being prepared for me in my heavenly resting place, may I* *fill that room with meaningful relationships here on earth. I pray for those I am close to and for those you put in my path. May I have enough influence in their lives to have them as part of my room. Amen.*

Is Grace Not So Amazing for You?

MOST THINGS MATTHEW does either make us laugh or cry. But whichever one we may be experiencing gives us the opportunity to learn something. Recently, Matthew started the morning frantically searching for a sock. A single sock. After summoning one of us to his bedroom closet to clear the multiple levels of security to be opened (which, by the way, needs another level), he found a prized sock and placed it on his hand. Unlike most triumphs where he completes something on his "list" of things to do, he did not make his normal happy noises. Instead, he went about his day with his socked hand raised up and out in front of him. We were quite curious to find out what was under the sock, but Matthew was not about to give up his sock and the mystery without a fight. It took a little restraint to hold him and to get a hold of the hand with the sock, which was writhing around and avoiding capture much like an anaconda. Upon removing the sock we found a small sliver of wood jammed under a fingernail. With a little coaxing (and more restraint) we were able to tweeze out the sliver. Matthew kept looking at his hand, first with concern, then with a smile and finally a laugh. The sock was tossed over the back of the sofa and out of sight. So simple. Do you have a problem, a pain or a concern? A little exposure and a willingness to ask and accept help is all it takes. Easy, right?

I have to confess, I have a sliver too. Actually, I have many slivers I try to cover with socks. Slivers, or sin, I purposely try to cover up and hide from an all-knowing God who is so desperately waiting with tweezers in hand. The only difference in this analogy is that God will not hold me down and restrain me. I have to come to a point of wanting change. It is then He wraps his arms around me, holds me tight, takes off the sock, and pulls out the pain.

I like a quote Dave Ramsey uses frequently on his radio show, which he also quotes in his book *The Total Money Makeover*. He is talking about money, but the application may easily be transferred to the stink of sin in our lives.

> *Change is painful. Few people have the courage to seek out change. Most people won't change until the pain of where they are exceeds the pain of change. When it comes to money, we can be like the toddler in a soiled diaper. "I know it*

*smells bad, but it's warm and it's mine." **Dave
Ramsey***

In his book *Humility: True Greatness,* C.J. Mahaney
talks about how sin bogs us down and makes grace
not so amazing. We become less impacted by
corporate worship or less sensitive to repetitive sin in
our lives. I think of the many ways I pull out a sock
and try to place it over the pain of sin. I think of the
ways I fill my life with being busy—busy enough to
not sit quietly and listen to the screaming coming
from under the sock. I ignore the fact God is
ALWAYS by my side, ALWAYS ready with the
tweezers. What are your socks? What do you use to
cover up sin? What do you use to quiet the throb of
pain? How do you find the strength to pull off the
sock?

I believe God had a plan in place when He gifted each
one of our children to us. With Isaac, it was to pull
us even closer to His embrace and His grip with the
tweezers in hand. Now since Isaac is home more
often than he is in the hospital, he requires 24-hour
observation and care because of his trachea tube
which requires constant suctioning to allow him to
breathe. We do get some help in the form of nursing
care at night, but I still get up at 6:30 a.m. to get a

briefing of the night. This is where my day begins, a full hour and a half to two hours before anyone else stirs in the house. God knew I would have much more focused time that I could choose to spend with Him. What could I do with this quiet time?

Dan Miller, an author and a person who has helped encourage and shape my writing and sharing of our story, frequently talks about the first minutes and hours of the day being pivotal in determining the outcome of it. He refers to this time as being the rudder of the day in a devotional book he put together of the same name, *The Rudder of the Day: Stories & Wisdom to Kick Start Your Workday.*

C.J. Mahaney also describes the first part of our morning as a time to speak truth to ourselves in opposition to the many lies we feed ourselves.

> *Most of us spend more time listening to lies than we do speaking truth to ourselves. And the listening process usually starts as soon as we get up. The alarm has rudely interrupted the gift of sleep, and the listening begins. As we stumble through our morning routine, we're not directing the thoughts in our mind—we are simply at their mercy. We entertain complaints about what*

happened yesterday and worries about what's coming today. We look in the bathroom mirror and assess the damage, then brood over how we feel. We're not in charge of our thinking. We are just there. **Humility: True Greatness, by C.J. Mahaney**

When and where do you take charge and take time to pull the socks off and allow the tweezers to come? As with Matthew, first there will be a look of concern, then a smile and then laughter as each sock is tossed aside.

Prayer: *Father, I commit to give to you the first part of my day. I pray that it will become my rudder of the day as I start in your Word and with thanksgiving and prayer. Lord, as I start each day with you, help me to reveal what is under the socks on my hands, and as each sock comes off may I experience your grace and forgiveness. Amen.*

In Good Times and In Bad

AS THERESA AND I entered the arena of raising a child with special needs, we were cautioned about protecting our marriage. "The marriage failure rate of parents with children with special needs is around 80–90%." we were warned. "These are cold, hard statistics," people told us. I think at the time we catalogued this in our memory and pressed on with the business of raising our children.

Theresa and I celebrate our 24th anniversary in October. I guess you could say we have gone against the odds according to what the statistics say. As I thought about this milestone, it made me think about what kind of trust I have in statistics. I began a search of where the 80–90% "statistic" came from, and frankly, I found much written about this mythical number, but not much evidence to back it up. Many have heard it, but I couldn't find anyone who could quote the source. In fact, many of the studies I found actually showed the numbers for special needs parents were less than the national average of marriage failures.

Theresa and I know firsthand the struggles of raising children, not to mention two of them with special needs. But marriage takes work, special needs or not. I believe failure or success is firmly rooted in the foundation of the marriage. The roots just have to be a little extra deep and a little extra wide for those with special needs children.

I started a new book once and didn't even make it out of the forward before something struck me and I had to write it in my journal. The book is called *Seeds of Greatness* by Dennis Waitly. Dennis' grandmother explained what seeds of greatness were one afternoon while they were tending the garden together, a common task they enjoyed and one which became a tool she used to pass on many life lessons.

The seeds of greatness are not dependent on a gifted birth, the inherited bank account, the intellect, the skin-deep beauty, the race, the color or the status. The seeds of greatness are attitudes and beliefs that begin in children as baby talk, as do's and don'ts, as casual family chatter, bedtime stories, locker-room gossip—as offhanded, almost unnoticed, delicately transparent ideas, like flimsy cob-webs, at first— then, with years of practice, become like unbreakable steel cables to shackle or strengthen our characters throughout the rest of our adult lives. **Seeds of Greatness, by Dennis Waitly**

I know the first few years with Matthew started in the flimsy cobweb stage and with years of practice we have become stronger, and so has our marriage. I won't try to convince you those steel cables are not tested and stretched, because we have our times of selfishness, whining, disagreements and pity-parties. But those steel cables we have formed are firmly anchored to the moorings, the foundation which was laid. Our foundation is the promises we made to each other and to our relationship with our Heavenly Father who blessed those promises.

One thing we have learned, which has held our relationship together, is the storms which test those steel cables will come to pass. They will come in everyone's life, relationships and families. An analogy about music puts the rainy, storm-filled days and the beautiful, sunny days into perspective. In music, the beautiful notes are separated by rests. The rests are just as important as the notes and cannot be ignored, because without them the beautiful notes cannot be noticed or enjoyed. Learning to play great music is learning to make smooth transitions

143

between the rests and the notes. I think it is the same in our journey with raising Matthew, Isaac and our girls. It's also the same in our marriage and our walk with God. We cannot forget that the storms are just as important as the beautiful days.

> *God left the world unfinished for man to work his skill upon. He left the electricity still in the cloud, the oil still in the earth. How often we look upon God as our last and feeblest resource! We go to him because we have nowhere else to go. And then we learn that the storms of life have driven us, not upon the rocks, but into the desired haven.*
> **George MacDonald**

How are your transitions from notes to rests and rests to notes? Do you need more practice?

Prayer: *Lord, help me to strengthen the cobwebs into steel cables that anchor me in the times of stormy weather in my life. I am grateful for the beautiful music when I can hear you at work in my life and in the progress of those you have given me to care for. Allow me recognize the "rests," knowing you are still at work while transitions are made into the next verse or chorus in my life. Amen.*

I Got Nothing I Asked For But Everything I had Hoped For

I HEARD A question which has made me look within and ponder the same question as it relates to my life. The question is: "If your life didn't include (insert trauma, life changing event, illness, etc.) how do you think your life would be different?" For me and my family, it made me ask the question, "If we didn't have Matthew or Isaac or both, how would our lives be different?"

This brought up a great conversation between Theresa and me as I asked her the same question. We both had the same answer. We both have never really thought of how it would be different. We have never really dwelled on what could have been. We both agreed, however, that we would not be the people we are today without the experiences we have had, good or bad, over the years since Matthew was born. We both agreed our life looked quite different from the "norm" when we had just four kids (before Isaac was born). With the addition of Isaac, our lives are now on a whole new level of different. With Matthew, we dealt with some medial issues, but mostly with behavior issues and feeling the need to constantly and vigilantly guard him for his safety. Isaac added a whole new level with his acute medical needs. I guess you could say we are well rounded now!

As I reflected on the question and how I would answer it, I recalled a post I wrote on our blog when Isaac was about one month into his three-month stay in the NICU. I thought it was relevant to the feelings I have been sharing, so here is some of what I wrote:

For those of us who pray, we quickly realize prayer is not just a request list of things we need or want, or think we need and want. I was shown a little perspective in a book I finished this past week titled: The Book of Man: Readings on the Path to Manhood *by William J. Bennett. It's a great book for fathers and mentors to boys and young men on the lives of famous people and not-so-famous people about what it means to be a real man of integrity, faith and one who leaves a legacy of worth behind when he is gone from this world. I was taken aback when I read this prayer included among the stories which were hand scribbled and found in a pocket of an unknown Confederate soldier at the end of the Civil War. It really made me think about what we pray for and what we think we should expect in return.*

146

I asked God for strength, that I might achieve;
I was made weak, that I might learn to humbly obey.
I asked for health, that I might do greater things;
I was given infirmity, that I might do better things.
I asked for riches, that I might be happy;
I was given poverty, that I might be wise.
I asked for power, that I might have the praise of men;
I was given weakness, that I might feel the need of God.
I asked for all things that I might enjoy life;
I was given life, that I might enjoy all things.
I got nothing I asked for but everything I had hoped for.
Almost, despite myself, my unspoken prayers were answered.
I am, among men, most richly blessed.
The Book of Man: Readings on the Path to Manhood, by William J. Bennett

Two lines echo in my head from this written prayer. "I got nothing I asked for but everything I had hoped for" and "I am, among men, most

147

richly blessed." This is where we are at right now in our early journey with Isaac. I know this prayer is serene and calm, but here is what it really looks like to us. Even among the meltdowns Theresa and I experience at different times during the week, the times we cry out and wonder where God is, the times we just cry because we have been strong for too long, we are still richly blessed. We have had the time to just sit in the dark with a tiny five-pound bundle on our chest, to listen and watch his tiny chest go up and down and to experience what is happening in and around one of the smallest of the new NICU rooms, room 338. What we see happening is Isaac's room continues to be a hub where nurses he has had along the way stop in to see how he is doing. We share conversations of how good God is and stories of how our church family is taking care of us, our home and our children. We hear how my blog is being shared and Matthew and Sarah Anne's fan base is growing as they have become staples around the third floor (and the gift shop). Where Hannah and Megan are referred to as the "big sisters" and we hear nurses talk about how they could only hope their kids will grow up with the same heart, sweetness, beauty and integrity. I got nothing I asked for but everything I had hoped for; I am, among men, most richly blessed.

Yes, we are frustrated with questions not being answered. We are tired, both physically and emotionally as we have been living a bizarre life of 10–11 hours a day divided between mom and dad at Isaac's bed and still trying to take time to be a family. I had a picture in my mind this week while I was driving, thinking about how it may have looked when Moses was leading God's people across the Red Sea. I imagined myself walking forward, but my head constantly looking side-to-side and seeing a wall of water being held back by the wind. I imagined those swirling winds above me and maybe feeling a spray of water once in a while. I see it, but I don't believe what is happening. What if the wind just stopped? What if I don't have enough faith in God to keep the water from surrounding me? All we can do is keep walking, keep moving forward and not think about the physics of how the water is being held back or how long it will be held back. We just need to trust that God is God and His word is His word and He will never leave us to drown.

What to pray for this week: decisions and a plan. We will be meeting with all the specialists and doctors at one time, in one room to discuss what to do next. Isaac's issue at this time, before we can move on to any other thing, is for him to be able to keep an airway open, period. We will look at some short-term solutions from mild intervention to more drastic ones such as a trachea tube. There has even been some talk about transferring Isaac to Mott's at the University of Michigan. This would put us at a whole new level of a "family disrupted," but we are willing to do it if it means moving forward.

Ultimately, please pray God's will is being done, that we will fulfill the reason God has chosen us to be here, that we continue to be strong, even in our own struggles to reach out to the many hurting people we run into here at the hospital and the families God placed in our pathway who we end up talking with, praying for and crying for. Pray for moms who are doing this on their own, teens and other siblings who are acting out, not knowing how to handle the emotions and fears which surround them as they deal with turmoil in their lives. Pray for families who have been here for many months, even moving to

Grand Rapids to be close to their child. Also pray that our little room, room 338, will continue to be a safe harbor for staff and doctors who stop in and chat, not knowing why they are drawn to Isaac's room. The door is always open…

I really can't add more than what I have already shared. Would our lives be different? We really don't care. We still have occasional meltdowns. We still cry out at times wondering where God is while cleaning smeared poo off the wall for the third time in the same day. We are content with being a conduit for God to show His power, His mercy and His healing. Even if the journey is hard. Even if the journey is sometimes painful. We have been called to this. We are richly blessed.

Prayer: *Father, I am thankful that I am richly blessed even though at times I may not be able to recognize those blessings. Thank you for giving me exactly what I need, not only what I ask for. You know my needs even before I know them and speak them to you. Give to me a desire to seek your will, not just my own wants and desires. Amen.*

37064780R00093

Made in the USA
San Bernardino, CA
09 August 2016